◆ HOW TO ROCK CLIMB ◆

Climbing
Anchors

◆ HOW TO ROCK CLIMB ◆

Climbing Anchors

John Long

CHOCKSTONE PRESS

Evergreen, Colorado
1993

How to Rock Climb: Climbing Anchors

COVER PHOTOS:

(front): Tom Borger and Jeff Perrin on Cosmos, El Capitan; photo by Greg Epperson

(back): Dave Bangston and Carla Zezula on Dangle Theft, 5.12c, Tioga Pass; photo by Chris Falkenstein

All uncredited photos were taken by Kevin Powell or Craig Luebben.

ISBN 0-934641-37-4

PUBLISHED AND DISTRIBUTED BY
Chockstone Press, Inc.
Post Office Box 3505
Evergreen, Colorado 80439

Other books by John Long:
Gorilla Monsoon
How to Rock Climb
How to Rock Climb: Face Climbing

Preface

In 1989, I authored the book *How To Rock Climb!* The commercial success of that manual, coupled with requests by both retailers and climbers for more, has convinced me to write several companion manuals. Whereas *How To Rock Climb!* spent a little time on a lot of subjects, these new books will cover in detail those subjects that deserve more attention.

The following material is specifically aimed at the rock climber, though the generic theories and various rigging constructs are no less relevant to the mountaineer. This manual does assume a reader's working understanding of the basic climbing system, including belaying methods.

Acknowledgements

In all fairness, this book should have four other names on it beside my own: Publisher George Meyers, whose idea it was in the first place, and who was left to do much of the work; Dona Tracy Salcedo, who edited and shaped the text (expertly, as usual); climber/photographer Kevin Powell, who spent most of the winter getting the photos just right; and climber/engineer/guide Craig Luebben, who spent several months scouring and shoring up the text and taking many additional photos. Without Craig's considerable and exacting contributions, *Climbing Anchors* would be considerably less than it is.

C O N T E N T S

CLIMBING ANCHORS

JOHN LONG

Why We Need Strong Anchors

Good, solid anchors are the foundation of technical climbing. They are required every time a rope is used and a pitch is led, both as protection and for belay anchors. Likewise, you cannot rappel or toprope without an anchor. Even now, with sport climbing dominating the climbing scene, where the bulk (if not all) of the protection is fixed, climbers still have to place anchors, belay, and slot the occasional nut – which brings us to an interesting predicament that many sport climbers face.

Up until perhaps 1980, even the most rabid aspiring climber had to work his way up through the grades. Sure, an exceptional "natural" might skip 5.7 and go straight to 5.8 or 5.9 routes, but he or she invariably spent some months, however few, on easier routes learning the ropes, as it were. It is precisely here, at the bottom end of the learning curve, that climbers traditionally learned the fundamentals of nut and piton placement, arranging anchors and all the rest. Now that bouldering has become a virtual sport of its own, and with the advent of climbing gyms, artificial walls, etc., climbers are skipping rungs and jumping onto grim routes much faster than before. Many of these tough routes are bolted bottom to top, and require nothing more complicated – per placing gear – than clipping bolts. However, because many of these climbers have launched onto the grievous routes without learning the art of placing protection, they may find themselves at a loss when they venture onto a difficult route that has no bolts – even though they are capable of the difficulty on a sport route.

However dazzling clip-and-go routes are, few climbers don't have aspirations to climb the Diamond or El Capitan, and fewer still eschew adventure climbing altogether. Yet "hardmen" from the clip-and-go scene often find their skills severely lacking when they jump out on the sharp end for real, having to place the pro on lead, arrange hanging belays with wired nuts, and so forth. In short, for many modern climbers, physical expertise often far outstrips experience with and knowledge of the technical climbing system – the ropes, the tackle and how it is properly used. A '90s climber might be able to flash a 5.12e sport climb, but might kill himself trying to get up the Steck/Salathé on Sentinel (5.9), because of his ignorance of the climbing system. Because of this danger, this manual (or one like it) has become an even greater necessity than in years past.

(opposite page)
Steve Schneider and Jeff Schoen on Excalibur, El Capitan.
photo: Chris Falkenstein

Because anchors are so fundamental to the climbing game, experience in setting single anchors and rigging multi-anchor systems (as in belays) is readily gained. Just the same, even experts make mistakes, and the results are sometimes tragic.

One of my first summers in Yosemite, I remember being down in El Cap meadow, organizing gear for a day of free climbing at the base of El Capitan. We noticed a three-man team up around the top of the Stoveleg Crack, about 1,200 feet up, apparently descending. The trio was huddled around a hanging belay point, fiddling with haul bags and ropes before another rappel to yet another hanging stance below. We thought nothing more about this, and finished packing our rucksacks. But as we started hiking toward the base, my partner Richard glanced up at the wall and suddenly said, "They're gone!" Gone?! I looked up, and where the trio had been but five minutes before, there was now only cold grey rock. I never learned the exact sequence of fatal events, only that the group had gained a two-bolt hanging belay, and instead of clipping off to the bolt hangers, they doubled the rope over the chain connecting the two bolts. Once all three climbers, haul bags and gear were hanging thereon, one of the bolts failed, the rope was no longer supported by the chain, and the three plunged to their deaths. Had they clipped separately to each bolt, the good bolt would have saved them.

Thus, the whole anchor need not rip out to produce a disaster. The failure of a crucial piece of protection also can be extremely hazardous. I remember the early years back at Tahquitz and Suicide rocks in Idyllwild, California. As we free climbed our way through each of the old aid routes, our options dwindled to only the most grim or improbable ones. As we pondered the possibilities, my friend Ricky had made a solo trip up to Tahquitz to scope out the Green Arch, an elegant, vertical arc on the crag's southern shoulder that for ten years had been a popular aid climb. When Ricky mentioned over breakfast one morning he thought there was an outside chance it might "go," climber Tobin Sorrenson looked as though the Hound of the Baskervilles had just heard the word "bone," and we had to lash him to the booth so we could finish our meal.

Since the Green Arch was Ricky's idea, he got first go at it. Tobin balked, so we tied him off to a Douglas fir, and Ricky started up. Following fifty feet of steep combat, he gained the arch, which soared vertically above for eighty feet before curving right and disappearing in a field of big knobs and pockets. If we could only get to those knobs, the remaining 300 feet would go easily and the Green Arch would fall. But the lower corner and the arch above looked grim. The crack in the back of the arch was too thin to accept even fingertips, and both sides of the corner were blank and smooth as polished marble. By pasting half his rump on one side of the puny corner and splaying his feet out on the opposite side, the vehement counter-pressure kept Ricky there – barely – both points of contact steadily oozing off because the wall was so steep and greasy. It was exhausting duty just staying put, and moving up was accomplished via a grueling, precarious sequence of quarter-inch moves. And the protection was piss-poor. Still, Ricky made it halfway up the arch before his legs gave out. He lowered off, and I took a shot.

After an hour of the hardest climbing I'd ever done, I reached a rest hold just before the arch arced out right and melted into the field of knobs. Twenty feet to pay dirt. But those twenty feet didn't look promising. There were some sucker knobs just above the arch, but clearly those ran out after about twenty-five feet, and would leave a climber in the bleakest no-man's land; nowhere to go, no chance to climb back right and onto the route, no chance to get any protection, and no chance to retreat. We'd have to stick to the arch. Finally, I underclung about ten feet up and out the arch, whacked in a piton, clipped the rope in and fell off. When Richard lowered me back to the ground, I slumped back and didn't rise for ten minutes. I'd ground a weeping strawberry into the left cheek of my arse, and my ankles were all rubbery and tweaked from splaying them out on the far wall.

Richard untied Tobin from the stout fir, whence he tied into the lead rope and charged up the corner like a man fleeing the devil on foot. He battled up to the rest hold, drew a few quick breaths, underclung out to the top piton and immediately cranked himself over the arch and started yarding up that line of sucker knobs.

"No!" I screamed up at him. "You're off route, Tobin. Those knobs don't lead anywhere!" But it was too late.

Tobin had the disastrous capacity to close his mind to all consequences and simply charge at a climb pell mell. On straightforward routes, no one was better. But when patience and cunning were required, no one was worse, because climbing, as it were, with blinders on, Tobin would sometimes claw his way into the most grievous jams. When he'd deadend and have to stop, with nowhere to go and looking at a Homeric peeler, the full impact of his folly and the horror of his predicament would hit him like a wrecking ball. Teetering out there on the very quick of the long plank, he would suddenly panic, wail, cry, and do the most ludicrous things. And sure enough, about twenty-five feet above the arch those sucker knobs ran out, and Tobin had nowhere to go.

The Green Arch,
Tahquitz Rock.

photo: Rick Accomazzo

I didn't think that piton I'd bashed under the roof would hold the fall Tobin was so imminently looking at. The next lower piece was some dozen feet below that pin, at a rest hold, so in truth, Tobin was looking at close to an eighty-footer.

As Tobin wobbled far overhead, who should lumber up to our little group but his father – a minister, a quiet, retiring, imperturbable kind of gentleman who hacked and huffed from his long march up to the cliffside. After hearing so much about climbing from Tobin, he'd finally come to see his son in action. He couldn't have shown up at a worse time. It was like a page torn from a B-movie script – us cringing and digging in, waiting for the bomb to drop; the good pastor, wheezing through his moustache, sweat-soaked and confused, squinting up at the fruit of his loins; and Tobin, knees knocking like castanets, sobbing pitifully and looking to plunge off at any second.

Now, there is always something to do, even in the grimmest situations, if only you keep your nerve. But Tobin was gone, totally gone, so mastered by terror that he seemed willing to die to be rid of it. Suddenly, he screamed down, "Watch me! I'm gonna jump."

We didn't immediately understand what he meant. Jump?

"Jump off?!" Ricky asked.

"Yes!" Tobin wailed.

"NO!!!" we all replied in unison.

"You can do it, son!" the pastor put in.

That was the worst possible advice, because there was no way he could do it. Or anybody could do it. There were no holds! But inspired by the pastor's tragic counsel, Tobin reached out for those knobs so very far to his right, now lunging, now hopelessly pawing the air like the falling man clasps for the cobweb. And he was off for one of the grandest falls I've ever seen a climber take and walk away from – a spectacular, tumbling whistler, arms flailing like a rag doll's, accompanied by a blood-curdling scream that would have turned the stomach of a statue. When he finally jolted onto the rope and we lowered him off, he lay motionless on the ground and nobody moved or spoke or even breathed. You could have heard a pine needle hit the deck. Tobin was peppered with road burns and had a lump the size of a pork pie over one eye. It's a miracle that the last pin, high in the corner, had caught him and had not ripped out as well.

Tobin sat dead still for a moment longer, then wobbled to his feet and shuddered like an old wet cur crawling from a creek.

"I'll get it next time," he mumbled.

"There ain't gonna be no next time!" Ricky replied.

This story provides an example of transcendental luck cheating the Grim Reaper of his rightful due (the piton that held Tobin's titanic pealer should have ripped out). Ocassionally, the climbing system is capable of heroics. However, I mention this story because it's the exception to the rule – whenever you expect miracles from the system, you're almost always in for a broken heart at the very least. This, unfortunately, was a crucial point lost on Tobin Sorrenson who, several years later, paid for it with his life.

The entire system of protecting and safeguarding the leader has been arrived at over a century of trial and error. Materials are no less refined than those used on the Space Shuttle, and designs are worked out on super computers. Still, every technological advancement has its limitations, and few sports are less forgiving than climbing when you push things beyond what can sensibly be expected, especially when these things are components of a system fraught with so many inherent variables. Equipment design might be an exact science, but using said gear in the field is not and never will be. Ultimately, it all boils down to experience and judgement. The most we can hope to do in this volume is familiarize climbers with the most judicious information and techniques.

It is almost impossible to conceive of the Green Arch scenario happening nowadays, what with the popularity of clip-and-go routes, and such a low priority put on gamesmanship. Yet a large part of climbing requires a sound understanding of anchors – what they are and how best to get them. I mentioned these anecdotes not to incite terror, but to stress the importance of good anchors, and to show what might happen if they're less than they should be. It matters little if an anchor fails on the top of a sport climb or on the twentieth pitch of the Shield, on El Capitan. It's big trouble either way. The purpose of this manual is to assist the climber in determining what is, and is not, a viable anchor.

For the novice leader, everything is new, climbing technique usually is lacking, confidence is low and fright is high. Because you are not familiar with the vertical environment and often are performing tasks for the first time, there are many doubts about the whole procedure – about how hard you actually can climb, about when you might err and plummet off the rock. For these reasons, sound protection is essential, and is your only safeguard against injury. Placing sound protection must be the first priority of any leader – buck novice, or twenty-year veteran. The fact that there are comparatively few accidents in climbing reassures us that protection not only works, but is easily placed.

While this book provides considerable information about climbing anchors, extensive practice on the ground, preferably in the company of a professional guide, is essential for the aspiring climber to safely enter the sport. Winging it out on the lead is a most dangerous game. Studying this book and other sources, plus taking an anchor clinic from a qualified guide, will enlighten you to the esoteric and oft-confusing world of anchors, and will greatly increase the security of your climbing adventures.

When you start setting your first anchors on a genuine

climb, double- and triple-check each element of the system. Analyze it like an engineer, bearing in mind the kinds of forces that could be generated and the possible directions of pull that could occur. Unless your partners are top-notch climbers (and even if they are), always eyeball their anchors like your life depends on them being "atomic bomb-proof" (because it does).

This book covers natural, chock, and fixed anchors, referred to collectively as simple anchors. It also shows how to rig simple anchors together to create complex anchoring systems, including oppositional anchors, equalized anchors, and toprope and belay anchoring matrixes. A selection of photos (with expository text) shows the right and the wrong ways to set up these anchors. Also, because webbing slings and 5.5MM cordage are used for rigging anchors and slinging chocks, I've included an evaluation of sling and cord materials. Otherwise, the focus of the book is entirely on rock hardware and its usage. Methods for connecting lead anchors into the protection system have not been covered in this book; refer to *How to Rock Climb!* for more detailed information on lead climbing protection.

I have not gone into the business of carabiners. This is a manual, not a tome – which it would be if I even mentioned all the hundreds of biners currently available. Remember that any viable biner – oval or "D" – is adequate for use in anchoring, providing the biner's specs have satisfied UIAA standards. Aside from freak occurrences, brand-name carabiners do not break. Everyone has their favorite make and model, but in terms of strength and safety, any good American or British-made carabiner will do the job and do it well.

Modern rock hardware is a sophisticated affair. The more elaborate devices have many moving parts, and a complete analysis would discuss fulcrum angles, logarithmic curves, micro clearances and a load of jargon particular to the engineer. Giving even moderate mention to these obtuse specs may delight the aspiring designer, but a load of graphs and bewildering terms are of questionable value to a climber interested only in what gear is out there and how it is used. Consequently, I've left any scientific investigation to the scientist, and have focused more on practical concerns. There is no end to the topic of anchors. There is always more than can be said. My aim has been to serve up the essential information, believing the endless variations and fine points are best learned on the rock.

A Brief History of Rock Hardware

What a difference 20 years makes! As recently as 1970, rock climbing was an entirely different – and much more dangerous – sport. Boots, or "Kletterschues," were poor performers. Ropes were adequate; but protecting the lead was a coarse business of slugging home pitons and slinging the odd horn. Artificial chockstones (aka "nuts") were available, but most were weird, funky widgets with limited utility. Save for really bombproof placements, these first nuts were far less reliable than pitons for securing the rope to the cliff.

This would be a typical British rack c. 1965 for use on Anglesey – hence the many pitons which were used for belaying only.

Photo: Ken Wilson

In 1970, most nuts were European imports. The best came from England, where they were invented. Initially, climbers were suspicious of nuts, and most everyone considered them unacceptable as a general replacement for pitons. Clearly they weren't as sound, and anyone making a hard sell for their use in the United States was accused of having European affectations – or of being a daredevil.

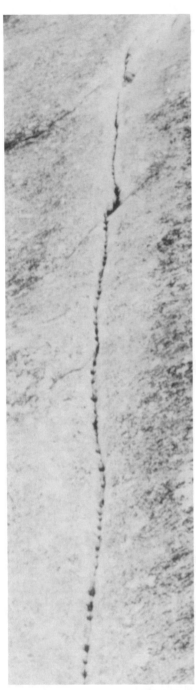

Piton scars on Serenity
Crack, Yosemite

Photo: John Stannard

Things changed suddenly. In the early '70s, John Stannard wrote a seminal article illustrating how pitons were rapidly demolishing the rock, and he suggested nuts as the only alternative if the crags were to survive aesthetically. Royal Robbins also drove home the point. Concurrently, Black Diamond (née Chouinard Equipment) began mass-producing chockstones, and almost overnight "clean climbing" became the rage. First "clean" ascents of popular big walls became fashionable. Climbers waxed poetic about "artful nutting" and "fair-means" climbing. By 1973, walking up to a free-climbing crag with hammer and pegs was akin to showing up at an Earth First! festival in a bearskin coat.

It is a good thing that the climbing community was won over quickly to clean climbing. The sport was booming, and every classic climb was destined to become a ghastly string of piton scars unless nuts replaced pitons as the common means of protection. Within a couple of seasons, clean climbing had reduced a climber's impact on the rock to chalk and boot marks. The benefits were clear, and the change was long overdue.

Unfortunately, the nuts available at the time still had serious limitations. Chouinard Equipment's "Stoppers" and "Hexcentrics" (both appeared in 1971) were pretty much the whole shooting match, though one could flesh out a rack with oddball European imports that did little more than take up room on the sling.

Recall that in the '70s, American climbing mores came principally from Yosemite, where cracks are generally smooth and uniform. The stoppers worked well in cracks that were ultra-thin up to an inch in width, but the first hexes needed a virtual bottleneck for a fail-safe placement. On long, pumping Yosemite cracks, such constrictions often are few and far between, if present at all. For several years, getting adequate protection from nuts was a difficult task. Ten-year-old test pieces became feared again, not so much for technical difficulties, but because of the lack of protection provided by available nuts. There were a handful of routes where you simply couldn't fall, though more than one climber did, and the scenes were not pretty. Clearly, the liabilities of these first nuts, coupled with climbing's ever-increasing standards, made clean climbing on hard routes a mighty bold prospect during that first phase of the hammerless era.

Then, in 1973, Chouinard changed the symmetry of the Hexcentric, eliminating the radical taper. The resultant "Polycentric" was a nut one could place three different ways, and each placement was far more effective than what could be achieved with the old design. These new hexes hinted at the camming to come, and brought a degree of security back to the sport.

Subtle changes also were appearing in other chocks. Wire cable replaced rope and sling for the smaller-sized nuts. Manufacturers entered the market with specialized gear–brass nuts, steel nuts, even plastic nuts were available for a short time. New-fangled homemade gear also began appearing, and the race was on for more diverse designs.

The pivotal breakthrough came in 1978, when "Friends" first became available commercially. The popular story is that Friends evolved from a simple camming device "invented" by Mike and Greg Lowe in 1967. Ray Jardine, a climber with a background in aerospace engineering, spent much of the '70s refining the concept (the Lowes had the right notion, but the actual device was almost worthless), and the first Spring Loaded Camming Device (SLCD) was the result. The era of super-specialized protection had finally arrived, and a protection revolution followed. In the ensuing ten years, SLCDs – or simply, "camming devices" — became available from many manufacturers in various forms and sizes. Also, component "sliding nuts" appeared which, because of their design, literally expanded in breadth when weighted in the direction of pull (this will be explained in detail later). Meanwhile, passive nuts were steadily improved and customized for specific applications. Sling materials likewise improved, as did carabiner design and rope technology. All told, the current state of rock-climbing equipment makes memories of barrel-chested bruisers in lug-sole boots slugging home pitons as quaint as memories of the Model T.

PART ONE:

Simple Anchors

The aim of this section is to address one-point anchors – a single nut, Friend, sling, fixed anchor, etc. – as opposed to combining single-point anchors into a matrix of solidarity. Adequate gear and suitable cracks are necessary to rig a decent anchor. Without one or the other, big problems arise. You might think the absence of good cracks would be the most dire, yet I recall a story from my friend and partner Richard Harrison that illustrates what can happen when the gear is lacking.

Richard and the late, great Nick Escrow were high on El Capitan when, moored at a hanging belay, Nick handed Richard the rack for the next lead. To their horror, the knot on the sling came untied, and the entire rack dropped into the void. That left them with about eight nuts and assorted pegs cribbed from the bottom of the haul bag, and the very anchor they were hanging from. They also were able to clean a couple of fixed pins, but the last pitches were extremely touch-and-go as they leapfrogged along, sometimes able to climb but fifty feet before having to stop and belay in a weird and perilous spot, sometimes "anchored" and hauling from one wired nut! Dreadful!

To the layman glancing through the following chapter on the various protection devices, the whole lot may seem bewildering and complex. Yet the basic use of protection usually is quite straightforward and self-evident. Simply put, you select a section of crack, and place in that crack a protection device of corresponding size. Since the size of the crack dictates what gear can be used, you instantly can eliminate all gear not in a specific size range. If you're looking at a half-inch crack, you have only to consider options that can possibly fit that crack.

In the absence of a crack – if the rock offers a suitable protruding or tunneling feature – or if a stout tree or bush exists, an anchor may be secured by slinging the "natural" feature. An ever-increasing number of face routes have been equipped with bolts, and obtaining anchors on these fixed routes requires only clipping into the bolt hanger.

*Chuck Pratt on El
Capitan's Shield Route*
Photo: Steve Sutton

Natural Anchors

Natural anchors consist of anything that the environment provides – trees, blocks, horns of rock, et al. Many times, a natural anchor is stronger than anything you could arrange with store-bought gear. Like any other anchor, there are numerous considerations that effect just how good, or poor, a natural anchor might be.

Of the many advantages of using sound natural anchors, three stand out. First, they are easy to use, in that most of the time, you can simply loop or girth a tree or a block (or whatever) with runners. Second, a girthed natural anchor is often bombproof no matter the loading direction. Third, natural anchors are the least environmentally disruptive means of protection.

Trees

Anchoring to a fifty-foot oak that casts a shadow like a thundercloud is pretty straightforward work. Judgement enters the game once the trees become smaller, and are located not on top of the cliff, but on ledges and shelves. I've seen some analyses of which trees are best suited for use as anchors that break down the matter so far as to studying the individual grain, but all this is an overstated stab at a question that basically boils down to common sense. Still, there are several considerations.

Some climbers think anything with bark on it is bomber, and the infamous Tobin Sorrenson was one of them. It was at Granite Mountain – not the gem in Prescott, but a scrappy little cliff outside Amboy, California that has for years been closed to climbing. (An old rummy with a 12 gauge full of rock salt stands guard, in case you're wondering.) Tobin was leading up one of those greasy, teetering slabs that look like you could make good time up it in Jap flaps, when in fact your only hope is to keep your $200 boots bicycling like Wily Coyote. When I clawed up to Tobin's belay and saw the anchor, I lost my mind.

"What the hell is that, Tobin?!"

"It's a tree . . ."

I'd shot pool with a bigger "tree" than this one.

"That's not a tree, it's a twig. A dead twig." And it was sticking out of a clump of orange moss on an angled, shaly little foothold stance. I reached over and yanked the sad thing out with about ten pounds of heft.

"Christ on high! You trying to kill us or something?!" Tobin cried.

The point being that what the tree is rooted in is probably

---

more crucial than the breadth of the tree itself. Good-sized trees have pulled out; the big one atop the first pitch of Catchy, at the Cookie Cliff in Yosemite, being a case in point.

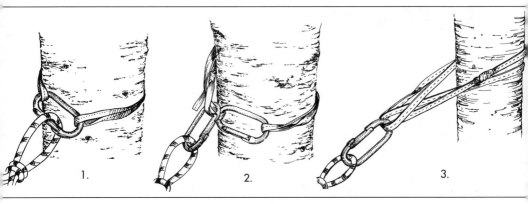

Anchoring to a tree:
1. Incorrect. This stresses the relatively weak gate of the carabiner.
2. Better, but the sling is overly stressed.
3. Best, especially when used with a locking biner.

Keep these points in mind. First, you want a live tree, preferably six inches or more in diameter, not one that's been chopped or burned or is rotten. Any tree rooted in shallow soil, gravel, scree, moss or soot, or that's burgeoning from a slim crack, should be considered suspect. If you've no other choice for an anchor – or even if you have – test the tree with a solid shake. Boot it, try to rip it out. If it still feels sound, it most likely is. Remember, of course, that a serious leader fall can generate much more impact force than a yank on the tree.

Whenever possible, tie the tree off with webbing instead of looping the rope around it. Once you get sap on a rope, there's no getting it off. Plus, the pivoting action common when leaning off the anchor can quickly abrade the sheath of a rope. Go with runners.

Unless the tree is truly a whopper, tie it off as low as possible to reduce the leverage. Never tie off a tree with a loop of biners. Girth-hitched runners usually are the first choice.

Shrubs and Bushes

Anyone who has tried to clear Grandma's backyard knows what a vile piece of work it can be to uproot healthy shrubs and bushes. Hence, they often make good anchors. As a general rule, it is easier and less time-consuming to rig a traditional anchor, providing one is readily available. But if good nuts are problematic to set, and a shrub, bush or sapling is at hand, use it.

Again, you want live stuff. Nothing brittle, charred, or loose will do. And make sure the stuff is well-rooted. Most of the time, a shrub or bush issues from a central root, and that's what you want to sling. Try to get the sling around that

---

whatever the feature...

- Look out for sharp edges.
- Test the security of the feature by thumping it with the heel of your hand. Anything that wiggles or sounds hollow is suspect.
- Look for surrounding cracks.
- Tie off as close to the main wall as possible, to reduce leverage.
- Tie off with runners, girth-hitching, or slip-knotting if the form is rounded.

---

fat root as near to the base as possible, and cinch it down snug. It is very sketchy to trust a solitary bush or shrub, and since they tend to grow in clumps, tying off to three or four (or more) and equalizing these anchors (to be explained later) is essential. More times than not you'll have to ferret around and push sometimes thorned limbs aside to get at the main root. Do so. Never settle for less than the best and least-leveraged tie-off you can manage. And always test the bush or shrub with a hearty yank.

Boulders and Blocks

These can provide sound, quick anchors if several things check out, and you follow a few rules of thumb. First, realize that both boulders and blocks are not part of the body of the cliff. They are detached, and the only thing keeping them in place is their size, weight and position. For a boulder or block to be any good at all, it must be both sufficiently big, and positioned in a way that it cannot be moved. It should not wiggle or budge at all. Anyone who has trundled boulders off a remote slab knows that a boulder big as a house can be sent on a path of mind-boggling destruction if it's on even the slightest grade.

Always tie off with slings. Avoid using the rope to reduce the chances of damaging it. Situate slings in a secure spot, preferably around a notch or constriction, where the sling is less apt to slip or shift. Try to tie the sling off tight, girth-hitching the formation. This is not always possible, and often runners get stuck, either by getting pinched under, or lodged between, the main wall and the boulder or block. Strive to avoid these situations, and watch for sharp edges.

Horns

I use "horn" here to denote all kinds of protrusions that one might possibly sling for protection. The various kinds are many: flakes, horns, spikes, chickenheads, bosses, bollards, etc. . . .

Flakes are simply shards or fragments of rock that are partly or completely detached from the main wall. Hence, it is the position of the flake that is our first concern. If the flake simply is pasted on a bald wall, it's very suspect. For a flake to be of any value as protection, it must be lodged in a manner that downward pull will only increase its security. Take the standard steps. Eyeball it. Is the quality of the rock okay? No matter how well the flake is lodged or jammed, if the rock quality is poor, it may snap in half if loaded. Thump it carefully, then harder if it's secure. Check for sharp edges. If you decide to sling it, understand that even the best-looking flakes often are unpredictable.

A quickdraw "thread," tied off directly with a runner. The thread is bomber, because the top of the knob is flush to the wall and the quickdraw cannot slip off. The rock would have to break for this anchor to fail. By hitching a runner directly through the quickdraw, you have eliminated a link in the system – a biner. If this setup was ever shock-loaded, however, the hitch on the runner would get cinched so tightly round the quickdraw you'd probably need a vice and a pair of needle-nose pliers to work it loose. Ultimately, the strength of this system hinges on just how strong the rock is. Be careful about threads in desert rock. Entire knobs can pop under the slightest load.

This marginal sling is slightly improved by setting a taper on the right to keep the sling in place. However, this rig looks pretty borderline on the left side. When a sling is simply draped over an edge like this, as opposed to being cinched tight with a girth or clove hitch, you want much more substantial purchase. Don't always expect to get it, however. Using the taper to shore up this placement has turned an unacceptable anchor into one that just might hold. But you wouldn't want to count on it. You're better off using the taper as an anchor, equalizing it with the sling. By loading it, you'd improve its ability to hold a sideways tug from the sling.

Blocks present the same problems as flakes, with added danger since they are bigger. If you should topple one off, you've essentially sent mortar fire down the crag and possibly onto your belayer. Position is everything. Look for a block that is keyed into place by the surrounding rock – lodged in a bottleneck is best. Loose blocks eventually slough off after a winter freeze, but they may remain perched, ready to plummet down the cliff under tread of a piss ant, for many years.

Spikes are pointed flakes or blocks that are usually, but not always, part of the main wall. On well-traveled routes, most of the loose rock has already been stripped away by previous parties, but don't bank on it. The first time I climbed El Cap, Ron Fawcett and I traversed the Grey Bands on the Nose, a weird, non-descript section at mid-height where the rock is grainy grey diorite. I was belaying from slings, and as Ron came up, I noted a thick, 300-pound spike just above me. It looked funky. I didn't know the numbers, but figured the Nose had been climbed at least 20 times by then, so all the loose stuff must have been long gone. Not so. When Ron grabbed that spike, it pivoted straight down, and I still don't know why he and the spike didn't land in my lap. The only things that had kept it in place were a couple of crystals and a slight updraft. The adage is: Never trust anything outright. Always assume it's trash, test it with caution, and only use it when you've convinced yourself it's good.

A boss is a rounded spike or knob; a chickenhead is a knob that often resembles a protruding mushroom; and a bollard is a hummock of rock. The bigger they are, the more probable it is that they are sound – but not always. Depending on the shape of the knob, the hardest part might be figuring out how to tie it off. The more rounded, the less secure. Use the girth hitch whenever possible.

Chickenheads must be approached with particular wariness. They usually consist of a mineral or rock type that is more resistant to weathering than the underlying stone. Carefully inspect the base of all chickenheads, because many are shot through with thin cracks. Thump them gently, then harder. I've had more than a few of them come off in my hands, and several have popped the moment I stepped on them.

Recreational climbers rarely venture onto new or infrequently traveled routes, where the above considerations are particularly germane. As mentioned, popular routes have long since had most of the loose rock booted away. But never count on it. Ultimately, common sense and a suspicious sense of judgement are your best weapons.

Threading Tunnels

When the rock weathers or cracks to form a hole in the main wall, climbers often can exploit the feature by threading a sling through the cavity. Common sense and sticking to the advice already laid down is key here. Is the feature strong? Thump it. Are there sharp edges? Is it cracked? And how big is it? Often, something as small as a suitcase handle can provide adequate protection. Anything less should be used cautiously, no matter how stout it appears.

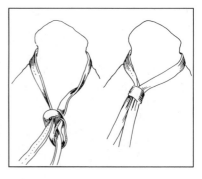

Slinging a horn with a slip knot tied into a runner.

Chockstones

Any rock lodged inside a crack is a chockstone. You appraise the security of the chockstone just as you would that of a nut – does the stone's symmetry correspond to the slot's? Is the stone set in a bottleneck or a constriction? Will downward loading decrease or increase its purchase? After considering these points, apply the same rules concerning horns, blocks, flakes, etc. . . . Are there sharp edges? What is the quality of the rock? If all things look good, but the positioning is suspect, wiggle the stone around and secure a better seating if need be, but be careful not to dislodge it. This is a very real concern with bigger chockstones.

Pay close attention to how you sling the chockstone. Often, even the slightest tension can cause the chockstone to wobble or rotate inside the crack, and the sling can creep between the stone and the wall and get stuck – or sometimes even pass between the stone and the wall. Chockstones are infrequently used because they rarely meet the above requirements, and often are problematic even if they do. Getting them well slung seems the hardest part. Again, the girth hitch is the first option.

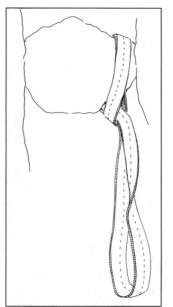

A chockstone must be girth-hitched on one side or the other to provide the maximum amount of security.

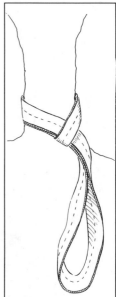

A tunnel girth-hitched with a runner

Hexes and tapers from
the early 1970s.

Passive Chocks

The family of climbing chocks can be split into two categories – passive chocks, which emphasize simplicity by having no moving parts; and active chocks, which achieve a high degree of utility through their geometry and moving parts. Passive nuts can be further divided into two categories: tapers, and all the rest. Passive nuts wedge into constrictions inside cracks, with the notable exception of Tri-cams, which can wedge in a constriction or cam in a parallel-sided crack. Perhaps the greatest asset of passive nuts is their simplicity. They have no moving parts, and are light, compact, reliable and easy to evaluate when placed.

As a primary anchor, it may be wise (but not always appropriate) to go with the low-tech, passive nuts – when you have a choice. They require less judgement, and are easier to evaluate with a novice eye. For instance, if the crack bottlenecks, place a taper in the bottleneck instead of wiggling a SLCD into a parallel section of the crack. Unless the wire fails (almost unheard of in tapers of medium size or greater), or the rock shears away (rare in good rock), there is virtually no way for the placement of a taper in a bottleneck to fail.

TAPERS

As illustrated, tapers basically are six-sided aluminum (or brass, or steel) wedges. The smaller sizes are strung with swaged cable. Medium and large tapers also generally are slung with cable, though some are machined to accept 5.5MM cordage as well. Note that one of the recent refinements in tapers is the elimination of overkill in the size of the wire. Instead of attaching a wire the size of a ship's cable, most manufacturers now are going with a thinner, lighter, less-expensive cable. The facts have dictated such a move – after all, given the quality of modern ropes, a normal-sized climber taking the longest possible fall cannot generate an impact force exceeding 2,420 pounds, so why employ a cable good to 5,000 pounds? Besides, using such a cable only adds weight and expense to the nut. Wild Country has noted that for years their tapers featured cable good to "only" 2,220 pounds, yet not one cable has ever failed in use.

The first tapers were much wider than they were thick. Now, virtually all tapers are of a much boxier design, particularly useful for end-wise placements. There are three basic variations on the original "straight taper:" the curved taper, the offset taper, and the micro brass or steel taper. In addition, designers have altered the sides of these various tapers. Some tapers feature gouged-out teardrop cutaways, or scoops. Some have been filed or beveled this way or that. The variations are many, but they are all meant to be slotted with the cable or sling pointing in the anticipated direction of pull. Ironically, most manufacturers have discontinued making the straight taper in anything but the smallest sizes, having found that the curved model is far more stable when placed.

Tapers often are the easiest nuts to place because the design is the most basic. The crack must pinch off in the direction of loading – usually down – to accomodate the taper. Simply try to place the taper that best corresponds to the geometry of the crack where it pinches (the so-called "bottleneck"). Ideally, you want a match fit, in which the contours of the crack are precisely those of the taper. Best of all is when the crack pinches somewhat in the outward direction as well. The very contour of the rock will resist a slight outward tug that could be created by a falling leader, or a belayer shifting about to get more comfortable. The ideal placement may be elusive as the blue moon or the perfect spouse, but good placements are generally plentiful.

Dealing with anything but the most deceptive placements really is a matter of common sense – you don't need to know a bag of tricks.

The more surface area contact you get between the rock and the nut, the better. Sometimes, you will have to slot a nut deep in a weird, flaring crack; but if you have a choice, place the nut where you can see exactly what it is set on. With straight tapers, you go after the bottleneck placements, or placements where the nut fits like it was milled just for that slot – the proverbial match fit. If neither of these placements are possible, try to firmly slot the nut in a constriction where the taper is lodged at about mid-range, or halfway up the faces. If the taper sets too low, say right above the cable, the nut is too big; if it is merely caught on the top 20 percent of the face sides, the nut is too small. Once again, go with the taper that best corresponds with the contour of the crack, and try to get as much surface area as possible on the rock.

Another consideration is size. If you have the option, go with the bigger taper. The cable is probably stronger, and the larger nut will afford more surface area contact and more security. But the principal concern is the placement – be sure the taper fits in the crack.

A large, straight-sided Chouinard Stopper set end-wise. This is usually inferior to the primary (length-wise) placement because of the decreased surface contact area of the taper, and the difficulty of finding a section of crack that perfectly corresponds with nut's taper. However, this crack was made for this nut – a match fit – with all of the nut's surface area in contact with the rock, and the nut slotted in the exact direction of anticipated pull (downward). This placement offers little resistance to an outward tug from the rope, though, so I wouldn't hang the farm on it alone. Set placements like this with a tug.

In shallow or flaring cracks, even pros have to tinker around to find the best placement, and this is where end-wise placements are most often used. An end-wise placement offers less surface area contact with the rock, but go with it if the fit is superior. You might have to, because many cracks simply are too shallow to accept a normal placement. Again, when the placement is marginal, look for that section of crack where the constriction best corresponds with the geometry of the taper. At times, you will have to try various tapers to find one that will fit at all, then have to jockey the nut around to locate the best placement.

Curved tapers are a bit trickier because they present options that straight tapers don't. A little more complicated, yes; but the fact that they have replaced straight tapers ten to one indicates the new design offers better stability in most placements. The actual curve is not very radical – usually just a few degrees – and normal placement usually attains a pretty flush fit on the face sides. You should always try to get this match-fit type of placement, but accept the fact that sometimes you won't.

A straight taper works much like a fist jam in a constriction, where both sides of the fist are lodged between the two walls of the crack. A curved taper sets in the crack like a hand jam, with three points of contact; a downward pull achieves a sort of rocker effect that further locks the nut in place. There are several things to understand about the curved taper design.

Another taper set end-wise. This archival Chouinard Stopper looks better than it actually is, because only the left side of the nut is in full contact with the rock. The right side is caught only on the top part of the taper. It is doubtful the nut would fail, but there is no doubt that if it sustained a longish fall, you'd have a devil of a time removing it. Because only part of the nut is lodged in the crack, that part is bound to deform, which makes cleaning egregious. Since the advent of SLCDs, and to rectify the cleaning problem, most climbers would place a camming unit (SLCD) in this situation. Also, this nut would be more compact slung with 5.5MM cordage.

This old Chouinard Stopper's placement, though not ideal, is sound. I'd like to see a little more of the right side of it in contact with the rock, but I'd also like to hear that a long-lost relative has just bequeathed me ten billion dollars. Understand that a textbook definition of a good nut is one you are unlikely to get all the time on the crags. You make do with what the crack affords, and what you have on your rack. This nut will do.

Take a banana. You can place it two ways on the table top, so the fruit curves one way or the other. Same thing with a curved taper. You have a "left" and "right" option, simply by turning the taper around. In a V-slot, or uniform constriction, the curved taper is placed the same as a straight one, and the curved design plays no meaningful role. Any nut will do in a true bottleneck. If a bottleneck or pronounced constriction is not to be found, you should find that section of crack that best corresponds with the taper's curve, and place it left or right as necessary for the best fit.

Very few cracks are perfectly parallel, and even the slightest wave or jag may be sufficient for the taper's curve. But when the crack is truly even-sided, you have to utilize the camming action of the nut. The crack still has to constrict, if only slightly, and you must go after that place where you can get a good three-point setting – a fix on the top and bottom of the concave side, and a firm lock on the convex side. Oftentimes, you must try both left and right placements before you achieve the best fit. The security of the nut, however, usually is determined by how much and how well the convex face is set. If the concave side has a decent, two-point attitude, much of the convex side is set snugly, and the rock below the point of contact narrows even slightly, the placement probably is sound. If the convex side is barely catching, or if its point of contact is either high or low, the nut most likely is marginal. Often, you can simply flip the nut around and get a better placement. If this doesn't work, you probably should go with another type of nut. If another nut – say an SLCD or a hex – still does not find good purchase, it's a judgement call which piece to use.

Beware that the crack doesn't open up on the inside; in this case, the chock could pull through and slip out below like so much sand through an hourglass. In horizontal cracks, try to find a spot where the crack opens in the back to accept a taper, but pinches off at the lip to hold it securely. Otherwise, place two tapers in opposition (to be covered later). Tugging on a precarious nut may set it and improve its stability, but tugging on every piece will drive your partners to hard drink as they curse and dangle from their fingertips trying to remove your stuck pieces.

A last and utterly critical consideration concerns the direction of pull – and this is relevant to all forms of protection, not only tapers. The question you must bear in mind is: In what direction will your plummeting body impact the nut? Obviously, gravity dictates that falling objects drop straight down. But chances are, your rope is snaking through a succession of protection below, and that the protection is not in a direct, up-and-down line. It most often is not. Consequently, in a fall, each nut is weighted by the rope, which holds the falling climber at the business end. Often, a falling leader will first impact a nut with a slight outward pull, then a heavy downward pull. Also, if the nut directly below the top nut is anywhere but directly below, the direction of pull on the top nut will be downward and somewhat toward that nut (at an oblique angle.) It sounds complicated, but it isn't, and the best and only way to determine the direction of pull is to consider the rock a geometric grid.

If you know where your protection is on the grid, you know that your lower nut is a little to the right or left of your top one, which means a fall will pull the top nut slightly to that side. After a couple of leads you will understand this simple principle. For now, it is important that you understand that protection should be placed appropriately for the anticipated direction of pull, or as close to it as possible. The cable or cord coming from the bottom of the nut should point in the direction of pull.

Bearing these points in mind, the business of making the difficult placement simply is a matter of jockeying the taper around in an attempt to best satisfy the aforementioned points. Accomplishing difficult placements is an acquired art, but it doesn't take a Fullbright scholar to realize a taper hung on a couple of crystals, hanging well out of a rotten crack is something less than bombproof.

This Wild Country Rock looks pretty cherry, and it probably is. Because the crack is smaller below the taper, the wire would have to break for this placement to fail. Yet, this is not ideal because so little of the right side of the nut is in contact with the rock. Here, "ideal" does not necessarily mean the placement will hold more of a fall, but rather that it will be relatively easy to remove if fallen on – a real consideration. When a nut of this shape sits on crystals, as this one does, it can get lodged for good if someone takes a good ripper on it. Even more importantly, a nut is more likely to wiggle out if it doesn't have good surface contact with the rock.

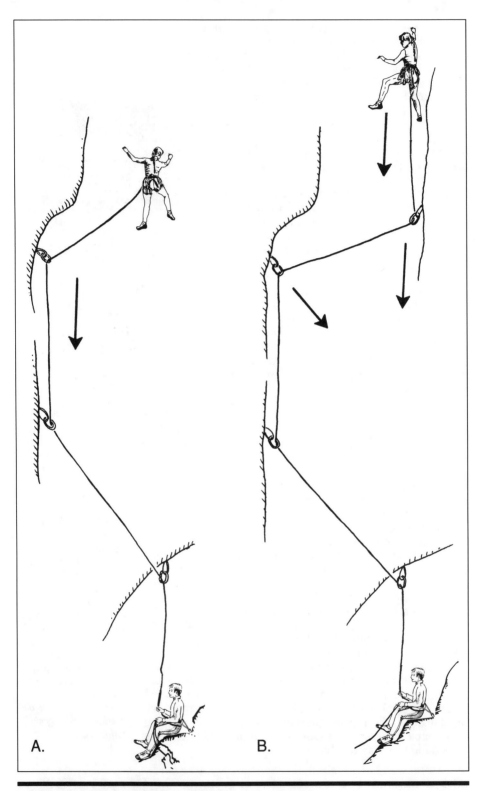

Offset Tapers

An offset is a comparatively new design, developed by Hugh Banner of the United Kingdom. These nuts are tapered in two directions, creating a shape that improves security in flared cracks.

The best way to understand this design is to get an offset taper and look at it. You'll find that one edge is thicker than the other – or "offset." Offsets are ideal for flaring cracks that narrow toward the back – like pin scars – where a normal taper would find scant purchase. Be warned, however, that though the offset will work wonderfully when properly set, it is less forgiving in marginal placements, and unless you've got most of the surface area firmly locked, offsets can pop faster than you can yell, "Watch me!"

Originally viewed as a specialty item for use on big aid routes, many free climbers carry a few for those "oddball" placements where nothing else works as well. They were first available only in small sizes; now that full-sized offsets are available, time will render the ultimate verdict on their utility.

Micro Tapers

Prudent use of micro nuts hinges on knowing their limitations. Regardless of what any catalogue might tell us, we know at a glance that a wee dollop of brass or steel at the end of a piano wire is, at best, a stopgap device – a last resort when the rock affords us nothing else. The limitations of micronuts are matters of strength – the strength of the cable, of the actual nut, and of the rock the micro is placed in.

Amazingly enough, cable strength is the least liability on all but the smallest micros. Cables on the puniest micros are rarely good beyond 1,000 pounds. Most manufacturers don't recommend them for free climbing, as even a short fall can snap the cables. But sizes beyond the smallest-feature silver-soldered or molded cables have wires that are good beyond 1,500 pounds and are adequate to survive falls of moderate length. The cables are fragile, however; frays and kinks denote weakening and are sure indicators that the nut should be retired. The cables are particularly prone to fray just beneath the body of the nut, a consequence of the wrenching they take when cleaning them from a climb. Place and remove them gently if you want them to last.

Both nut and rock strength are the significant limiting factors of micros. Look in any catalogue featuring micros and you'll see many disclaimers and explanations. The language can get confusing, so let's look at it in simple terms.

basic rules of placing a good taper

- The taper has to be bigger – if only a bit – than the section of crack below where it is lodged.
- Slot the taper that most closely corresponds to the geometry of the crack.
- Whenever possible, set the taper where the crack not only pinches off in the downward direction, but also in the outward direction.
- Orient the taper so the cable or sling points in the expected direction of pull.
- Try to get the majority of the nut set against the rock, maximizing the amount of surface contact.
- Avoid end-wise placements if possible, as they tend to be less secure.
- If you have a choice, go with the bigger taper, as it tends to be more secure, with more surface area touching the rock.

(page opposite)

The direction of pull on protection changes with the next placement. In figure A, the falling climber will impact the protection straight down. Figure B shows how a fall on protection placed higher will change the direction of pull. Note that the falling climber will not pull entirely straight down on the top piece because of the placement of the previous nut.

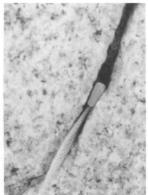

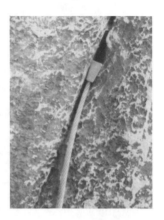

This HB Offset looks funky. Only the top left side is touching rock, and the right side is hunkered down on a few bumps. Again, because the crack narrows below the placement, it might not fail. But remember this: The smaller the nut, the more you want a match fit in which most, if not all, of the nut's surface area is in contact with the rock. A little rope wiggle might send this sliding back down the lead rope.

Friends, this is about as good as it gets for a nut this tiny. As is often the case, this RP has found its natural home and appointed rest in a pin scar, the sides flush with the crack, the crack below thinner, but not so much as to thwart the run of the cable. The only improvement would be to find the same placement in a perfectly vertical crack, because even nominal cross strain on the slender cable is unwanted. It also would be nice if there was a little more pinching on the outside edge of the crack so the piece definitely couldn't wiggle out. But this is, after all, textbook talk, describing a placement you want but rarely get.

I wouldn't want to run it out on this stinker! The right edge of this micro projects from the crack, so even the slightest rope movement can dislodge it. A slight tug to set it is warranted. Tug too hard, however, and you risk cable deformation and curses from the person who must remove it. Count too much on placements like this and you're likely to see the ground rushing up fast.

Regardless of type or brand, the actual nut head on any line of micros is indeed micro. When you fall – and eventually you will – your weight impacts a very small piece of stainless steel or brass. Depending on how malleable the nut is, and how hard the rock is, several things can happen. With stainless micros, even when placed in flint-hard granite, a moderate fall should not radically deform the nut's shape, because the relative hardness of stainless steel is quite high. However, if you place a stainless micro in quartz monzonite (Joshua Tree) or sandstone, where rock is prone to shearing away, even the perfectly placed stainless micro can rip out, leaving a little groove where it literally tore through the rock. If the rock is something less than granite or dense limestone, brass micros don't tend to rip out, because the softer brass can deform and bite into the rock. In soft rock, brass micros tend to seat better than stainless because of increased

Holy mackerel, Andy! I wouldn't hang my hat on this dud. Though this is the type of placement that these boxy-shaped micros were designed for – and indeed, this is a "good" placement, with a match fit, room for the cable, etc. – this nut clearly illustrates the shortcomings of micros. First, it's hanging on the very outside of the crack. Any movement, and it's out. The cable, though slender, is stiff, so scant rope drag could lever the nut out in a heartbeat (unless it's well-seated with a tug). And since the nut is placed askance to the probable direction of pull, which is straight down, a fall would bend the soldered cable just below the body of the nut. The nut will sit crooked on the cable till it is bent back. You can only bend and tweak the cable around so many times before several or more of the small strands break. Understand that micros work better than you would think, but they are fundamentally fragile, and are often retired after sustaining a couple of falls, if that many.

A-1! This bottleneck placement is somewhat rare for a wired micro, as the bottleneck does not close down thinner than the wire. Though the nut's sides are not totally touching the crack, the bottleneck prevents it from being pulled out sideways. The cable would have to break for the placement to fail.

Because of their boxy shape, near parallel-sided cracks often afford the best placements for micros. Careful placement is essential, because the relative differences between a good and bad micro are very small indeed. While it is tempting to slot the nut deep in the crack, it's usually better to keep it fairly close to the lip, where you can see just how good, or bad, the placement is. The right edge of this HB Offset appears to make good contact with the rock, but it's difficult to see exactly what is happening on the left edge. It's troublesome to accurately assess this placement without getting a closer look. Get your nose right in there and check out the placement thoroughly.

friction and bite. In diamond-hard rock, however, softer micros sometimes can't offer enough resistance to the impact force of a stout fall, and they rip out. It's a trade-off, and most climbers own a variety of micros for different situations.

This HB Offset appears to make good contact with the crack walls, and the lip at the edge of the crack will help hold it in place. If the rock is solid, this nut is sound. But because it is a micro nut, you'd want to back this piece up when possible.

This HB Micro Anchor appears to make perfect contact with the rock, and even looks somewhat stable against an outward tug. You'd be hard-pressed to find a better placement for this dinky piece.

A "load-limiting" quickdraw, such as the Yates Screamer, can increase the safety margin of micro nuts, or any other dubious gear used for lead protection. The Screamer has tear-away stitching that activates at 500 pounds to absorb the energy of a fall to limit the impact force on your protection.

A couple things to remember when placing micros: Anything but a match fit, where most all of the nut's surface area is flush to the rock, should be considered a marginal placement. The four sides of some micros are nearly symmetrical. For those that aren't, end-wise placements should be slotted with a prayer.

Place the micro directly in the line of pull. The relative clearances of even an ideal placement are quite small. Lateral torque can pivot a micro right out of the crack.

Always extend the placement with a quickdraw, rather than clip a biner straight into the wire. Even marginal rope drag can lift the micro from the crack. Try to avoid placements where the wire is running over any kind of edge. Do not wildly jerk the micro, either when setting or removing it, lest you prematurely bend, weaken, or even break the wire.

If a micro is the only nut separating you from eternity on bleak terrain, you are mad, and should offer novenas before casting off.

Offset micros always should be considered trick, or specialty nuts. As mentioned, it is highly advisable to go after the match fit. Micros have precious little surface area to begin with, and you want all of it flush to the rock. This is even more essential with offset micros. If the sides of an offset micro are not lodged fast, it will pivot out when weighted. I learned this the hard way on El Capitan, and took a thirty-foot fall in the process.

Like the larger offset tapers, offset micros are particularly useful in pin scars, where the bottom of the hole is flared and a normal taper would be lucky to just hinge on a couple of crystals. Offsets can lock right into these placements, but you must be able to visually verify the match fit. If you can, offsets are remarkable.

ALL THE REST

Tapers are designed specifically for small cracks, and are indispensable for cracks up to about ¾-inch wide. The smallest are about ⅛-inch thick, the largest about 1¼-inch thick. Beyond these dimensions, the design becomes prohibitively heavy, and other designs – "all the rest" – take over.

In larger cracks, active camming nuts generally offer more utility than passive nuts, but the larger passive chocks, such as Hexentrics or Tri-cams, can be useful to complement active nuts, particularly on a large rack, or as an economical option for toproping.

Originally, Chouinard's Hexentrics (and later, Tube Chocks) were the sole option for medium to wide cracks.

Now, there are several other designs, though camming devices have for the most part replaced "all the rest" as the nut of choice for medium to wide cracks.

Hexes

Because the sides of a hex are angled similar to the opposing faces of a taper, you generally can place them using the same rules of thumb that apply to tapers. You want that match fit, in which as much surface area as possible is flush on the stone. If you look at a hex, you will see it affords two possible placement angles, plus a third if the nut is placed end-wise. Chances are, one of these attitudes is going to work if the crack constricts at all.

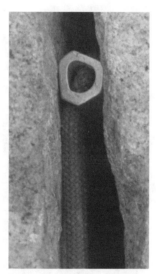

A bombproof hex. Much of the nut's surface area is flush to the rock, and the nut's symmetry fits the crack. It is not lodged near the lip of the crack, nor is it so buried that cleaning will be grievous. As good a hex as you'll ever get. Sling the nut with Spectra or Gemini cordage (rather than the perlon used here) to increase strength and decrease bulk.

A match fit for this hex; it's flush with the crack, in a slight constriction, and near the lip for easy removal. Since the nut is not in a bottleneck, however, its placement is prone to wiggling out with even nominal rope drag, as are similar placements. Set the nut with a good tug. The holding power is not in question, only getting the hex to stay put. Remember, if the crack was just a slightly more parallel, the nut could slip down into the opening below.

A bottleneck hex. Both sides of the hex make complete contact with the rock. Provided the direction of pull is downward, this nut is virtually fail-safe.

Tri-Cams

The beauty of the Tri-cam is its ability to work in both parallel and constricting cracks, and its uncanny knack for fitting where nothing else can. The Tri-cam design is meant to create a stable tripod with the two parallel camming rails flat against one side of the crack, and the fulcrum point contacting the opposite side. For placement in parallel-sided cracks, Lowe Alpine, the manufacturer, advises: "Cock the Tri-cam by wrapping the sling around the body, so it lies between the two cam rails. Find a slight rugosity or hole to place the fulcrum point in, then lay the rails against the other side of the crack. Set the Tri-cam with a tug."

Rock hardness, crack taper and flare will affect the security of a given placement. If the placement is prone to sideways or outward pull, sling the Tri-cam, or extend it with a quickdraw. Some practice is necessary to judiciously place

  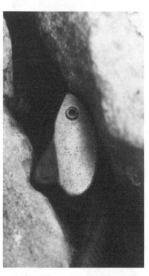

A well-placed Lowe Tri-cam set in the "taper mode." This piece should remain stable in its placement. If you fall on this one, though, it will be rugged to get out.

The crack is a bit too parallel for the Tri-cam to be used like a taper, and it seems to open up just below the piece, which is kind of spooky. A smaller Tri-cam set in the "camming mode" would be better, or perhaps this one could be cammed with the point seated in the depression just below the piece. An SLCD might be the best bet here.

The fulcrum of this Tri-cam sits in a piton scar, which improves the stability of the placement. However, this piece might fall out if it receives a lot of sideways rope wiggle.

the Tri-cam with one hand. The unit is considered a somewhat esoteric specialty item by many climbers, but those who climb rock heavily featured with horizontal, seamy cracks, or pockets and huecos, swear by them. Tri-cams are particularly useful in areas like the Gunks because when they are buried in a horizontal crack, only a soft sling runs over the lip of the crack, as opposed to a cable.

The smaller Tri-cams – #0.5 through #2 – are the most useful and the most stable. Used as belay anchors, they allow the climbing team to save SLCDs for the lead. At 9.4 ounces, the largest unit is quite a load, and the larger units tend to be less than perfectly stable. My only strong criticism of the Tri-cam is that its slings cannot be readily replaced, unless you send it to a company such as Yates Gear that professionally replaces the slings.

The Tri-cam's ability to literally bore into soft rock and avert diaster is best illustrated by another story from the field. Craig Luebben informs me that one of his most terrifying moments came on the second ascent of the beastly Silmarillion, in Zion Canyon. Craig writes: "I was groveling up a sandy piece of desert offwidth, ready to pitch off, with only a #7 Tri-cam between me and my belayer seventy feet below. Suddenly, the Tri-cam popped out and caught on my boot. Eying the chopper ledges in my landing zone, then the ground some eight-hundred feet below, I squirmed like hell to fetch the Tri-cam. I had no other gear to fit the crack, and down climbing was out. After some world-class squirreling, I finally snagged the piece, reset it and fell. I frigged the rest of the lead, afraid to move an inch above the precious but shuddering Tri-cam." Craig had no sooner finished the route off, than he went back home and invented the Bigbro.

Bigbros

The Bigbro is a spring-loaded tube of 6061 aluminum for use in wide cracks. Its minimum breaking strength is over 3,200 pounds. Four sizes provide an expansion range from 3.2 to 12 inches.

Craig Luebben of Mountain Hardwear, the manufacturer, is a throwback – a climber who actually enjoys offwidth cracks and chimneys.

What started out as a "senior honors thesis" for his engineering degree has been refined into the most effective – and virtually the only – mode of protection on the market for cracks bigger than 6.5 inches. The Bigbro appears to be simply a spring-loaded tube chock, but it's much more than that. I won't go into detail because it would take three pages to explain exactly how this sophisticated piece of gear works. Though it takes some preliminary fiddling and experimenting to get the knack of placing a Bigbro quickly

This Mountain Hardwear Bigbro is well set in a small parallel section of this flared crack. With the ends of the Bigbro solidly in contact with the rock like this, and with the collar tightly cinched, this placement will hold any direction of pull.

and correctly, each unit comes with a pamphlet on use, and a climber can get the hang of it in a matter of minutes.

A set of four Bigbros weighs nearly two pounds, and will set you back about $250, but they work like magic, and the alternative is nearly always no protection at all. The #2 Bigbro alone provides nearly the same expansion range as an entire set of the old Chouinard Tube Chocks. For wide cracks, the Bigbro is as revolutionary as the first Friends were for smaller cracks.

Removing passive chocks

To remove passive nuts, first try a gentle approach, simply wiggling the piece out the way it went in. If a taper is stuck, you might try a slight upward tug – but remember, jerking in any direction other than straight down from the bottom of the nut may kink or even break strands of the cable (resulting in hateful "wild hairs," little filaments of sharp cable that can and will prick your chafed fingers like porcupine quills). If the piece still won't come out, try loosening it with increasingly harder nudges from a nut tool. Thin, blade-shaped, and available in a dozen forms, nut tools are invaluable for releasing a stuck chock. If a taper seems to be profoundly stuck, place the end of a nut tool against the wedge itself, and tap the other end of the tool with a large nut, fist-sized rock, or other object. If the piece moves but won't come out, it's a matter of fiddling with it until you stumble across the same path and orientation in which it was placed. If the piece won't come, better to leave it before you completely trash the cable, so it will be of use to future parties. Someone more crafty or persistent might be able to clean it from the cliff.

Mechanical Anchors

In contrast to the simple looks and easily understood what-you-see-is-what-you-get mechanics of passive chocks, the high-tech gear described in this chapter would impress Rube Goldberg. The bottom line, however, is that they work great, especially in places where nothing else can.

SPRING-LOADED CAMMING DEVICES (SLCDs)

The only way to get an adequate picture of an SLCD is to get one and study it. Briefly, all SLCDs are shaped similar to a capitol T. The top (horizontal) part of the T features a solid axle on which are arranged either three or four opposing, teardrop-shaped lobes. The vertical part of the T is the stem (there are both rigid and flexible-stemmed SLCDs), which has a triggering device that allows you to adjust the span of the spring-loaded lobes. Each unit has a minimum and maximum degree of latitude, and each is adjustable within those parameters. With a full selection of SLCDs, you have a rack that can be micro-adjusted to perfectly fit just about any size crack from about ⅜-inch to 6½-inches. Again, it's best to get several of these units in hand to understand fully how they work. Once you understand the basic principals, SLCDs are perhaps the easiest, most functional, and certainly most adaptive pieces of equipment on your rack.

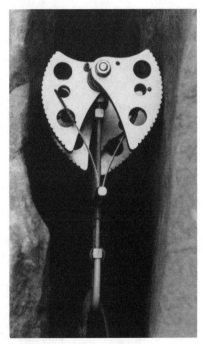

    Historically, the advent of the SLCD marked the start of the protection revolution, and in terms of gear, was rivaled only by the development of "sticky" boots in the technical advancements of the sport.

    I still remember the great secrecy that surrounded the arrival of the original "Friend," the first commercially viable SLCD (the Lowe brothers sold one briefly, but it performed so poorly it quickly disappeared). They were developed over a period of several years by Ray Jardine, a climber as peculiar as he was talented. Ray always had to enlist other climbers for his many projects throughout Yosemite, ventures done with all the stealth of a coup de'etat in Haiti. The real secret, however, was not the new route, but the strange gear on Ray's rack. Partners were sworn to secrecy over Ray's prototypes, and Ray made them do everything but sign a contract in triplicate that they wouldn't filch the concept (as

A well-placed Yates Big Dude in a four-and-a-half-inch crack. The cams are at mid-range and the unit is aligned for a downward pull. Good enough.

This Friend is too small for the crack; this is obvious because the second lobe from the front is "tipped out." As mentioned, when the lobes are at or near the limit of their possible breadth, the unit is considered marginal. Even the slightest rope drag can pivot the piece enough for the lobe to invert, like a sprung umbrella, rendering the unit worthless. Often, you can jockey the unit around and find a better placement. If not, use a bigger unit. Fact is, you climb long enough and you'll inevitably have to make just such a placement. The crack will be just this size, and the only unit left on your rack will be too small. Place it, trying to find the narrowest place in the crack. It may hold. But understand that you are hoping the unit performs beyond the specs it was designed for.

Ray had done from the Lowe brothers years earlier), tool up, and start cranking out the new-fangled widgets for commercial ends. I remember John Bachar climbing halfway up the East Face of Washington Columm to try to clean a fixed Friend. He got it, too. The next year, we all had them, and Ray retired to the South Pacific on his eighty-foot schooner. Never saw Ray again.

In short, SLCDs work by translating a downward/outward pull to an even larger force against the walls of the crack; this in turn creates friction between the rock and the nut, thereby resisting the pull. (Just get one and look at it, and all will become clear.)

The most obvious advantage of SLCDs over passive protection devices is the speed and relative ease of placing them in a crack. But just because you can get almost instantaneous placement does not mean the protection is any good. The great majority of SLCD placements are sound and pretty straightforward, but for those tricky placements, it is essential you know the limitations of the devices, as well as some general rules of thumb that apply to all camming units.

SLCDs fall into two categories: four and three-cam units. Four-cam units have two sets of opposing lobes, or cams, situated along the axle, whereas three-cam units feature a single middle cam opposing the two outside cams. Four cams provide the best strength and stability, while three cams reduce the unit's profile to allow placement in shallow cracks.

Any camming device is "flexible" if the stem is not rigid. There are several reasons why flexible camming devices were invented. First and foremost, a rigid stem is a liability in pockets, and in horizontal, diagonal or shallow placements. When odd angles or torque is involved, a fall can wrench the unit in strange ways, bending or even breaking the rigid stem (the latter is very rare), or – more commonly – ripping the unit out of the rock. In thin placements, the thicker rigid stem gets in the way, and often the stem is thicker than the crack, making placement impossible. A cable stem gives the unit a thinner profile and greater options for application.

Also contributing to the development of flexible camming technology is the matter of economics, and the trigger design patent on rigid-stemmed devices held by Wild Country. Individuals who wanted to make camming devices couldn't afford to tool up like a big company. By using cable (which was inexpensive and readily available in small amounts), they eliminated a machined or cast part, and were able to create a trigger design that didn't infringe on Wild Country's patent. Oddly enough, these monetary hardships and patent considerations led to many of the refinements in flexible camming devices, because budding manufacturers were left to solve problems creatively, rather than by throwing money at them.

It is not entirely fair to contrast rigid-stem camming devices with flexible units because the applications are different. Rigid units won't work in ultra-thin cracks because the stem is too big. Flexible-stemmed units generally will work fine in wider cracks, however – though not as well as rigid units. But to claim a flexible unit cannot provide adequate protection in anything but thin cracks is patently untrue. The issue becomes more involved with flexible units that feature a double stem. Though indeed flexible, they offer more stability than a single cable stem, but still are less predictable (in terms of loading the cams) than a rigid stem. Because of these variances, one should know this much about flexible camming devices:

1. They are less durable than rigid units. Under the impact of a fall, the cables can kink and/or become permanently deformed.
2. It is impossible for a flexible cable to load the cams as predictably as a rigid stem does.
3. The action of the flexible units is less positive because of the inherent flex. This can make placement and removal more difficult, particularly when a climber is fagged.

In terms of use, differences between rigid and flexible-stemmed camming devices are obvious. The rigid devices load the cams more predictably, and testing has suggested that for generic use, rigid devices have a strength advantage over flexible-stemmed units. Different makes have different specs, of course; but all American or British-made SLCDs employ quality materials and craftsmanship, so the relative strength of rigid-stem versus flexible-stem often is overstated. Rigid-stemmed units cannot be placed where the impact of a fall will stress the stem other than along its vertical axis. For instance, in a horizontal placement where the stem is set over an edge, a fall will bend or even break it. These placements are to be avoided.

The promotional materials on SLCDs can be misleading – even outright nonsense. The real question is not the absolute strength of the component materials, but how well the device holds in the crack. Since most tests are conducted in a shop (using a jig), and because the rock affords a virtually unlimited variety of placements, most of the testing can only prove the strength of component parts (the axle, etc.), as opposed to how well the unit will perform in the field. Consequently, shop tests only tell us so much. It should be noted that a properly placed SLCD very rarely breaks. It's almost unheard of that a fall has reduced a device to a glob of bent cams and blown-out springs. Most often, the unit has simply ripped out of the rock for any number of reasons. Thus, when you read fantastic claims of "stronger" SLCDs, the propaganda is referring to the component parts, and not the unit's effectiveness under the stress of a fall out in the field.

A made-to-order crack for this Black Diamond Camalot. The individual lobes are at mid-range, and the device is set deep enough that even if it walks, or pivots up, it will not come out. Always watch for cracks in the wall, like the tiny crack to the right of the Camalot, which brings into question the rock's stability. This placement is probably fine, but all the same you could place it a couple of inches higher to be absolutely sure.

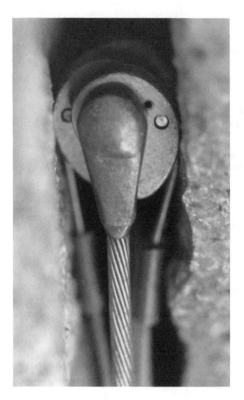

Note that the lobes on this Metolius TCU (three-cam unit) are at about mid-range. The crack is parallel-sided, and the unit is close enough to the lip that you can eyeball the placement, yet deep enough that pivoting won't dislodge it. A sound placement.

Not an ideal fit for this Friend; a bigger unit should be tried, or this piece should be moved to the right, where the crack is a little tighter. The inner lobe on the left side is nearly maxed out, but the others look better. Flexible-stemmed units were designed for horizontal placements like this. Given that a climber will probably pass over this placement, or will belay below it, the loading direction is straight down, and any load could bend or tweak a solid-stemmed unit like this one. Here, the problem has been solved by tying the unit off short – running the tie-off loop through one of the holes on the stem above the trigger. Understand that even when all things check out, horizontal placements tend to be the most problematic for SLCDs.

Each cam on every SLCD is individually spring-loaded - regardless of whether it's a three- or four-cam unit or equipped with a rigid or flexible stem. The degree of expansion or contraction of one cam is not affected by the position of the other cams. This allows the unit to accommodate size irregularities inside the crack with little loss in stability. The first camming unit, the Friend, was designed to provide quick protection in parallel-sided Yosemite cracks. But there are plenty of other climbing areas outside Yosemite, and most cracks are not parallel-sided. When the inside of a crack is even slightly wavy, the individual cams on SLCDs will adjust automatically to the irregularities. That is, the cams will be deployed at varying widths. When this happens, as it often does, certain things must be remembered to ensure sound placement.

Though most camming devices feature a constant, or nearly constant angle at which the cams meet the rock throughout their expansion range, the safest and most secure placement is when the cams are in the lower half of their expansion range. Be careful, however, not to stuff a piece into the tighest placement it can fit, lest you must sacrifice a $50 piece as fixed gear. In an irregular-sided crack, maneuver the unit around so the cams are deployed as uniformly as possible. Remember that even moderate rope drag can cause the unit to "walk," or move around in a crack. In a really wavy crack, even meager movement can radically alter the position of the cams, and render the placement poor, or even useless. Trying to get placement where all the cams are about 10 to 50 percent deployed will give you some leeway if the unit walks. If the cams do open more than halfway, try the next bigger size.

There are several configurations a camming unit can assume that spell danger – or at least trouble. As mentioned, one of the most troublesome positions is when the cams are fully closed inside the crack. That means no matter how hard you pull on the trigger, you can't suck the cams in any tighter, you can't loosen the unit, and you probably can't get it out. It is not unheard of for excessive rope drag to put enough tension on a unit that it walks itself into this fully-closed position, but it is rare. Much more common is the situation in which a frantic climber shoves too big a unit into too small a crack. Sure, the unit will most likely hold a fall, but removing it probably will entail holding someone on tension so both his hands are free to spend a good long time cursing and jerking the unit this way and that. To avoid the hassle of battling with stuck SLCDs, make sure to place a unit that fits, again with the cams between 10 and 50 percent deployed.

With the smaller camming units – ones with a very limited expansion range – particular care must be taken to avoid getting the unit stuck. You have much less room for error, as the cams only expand a little. With these smaller units, you must make placements with the same precision as with a tricky taper placement.

Once you realize a SLCD might be stuck, be careful how you work with it — frantic jerking can turn a mildly stuck SLCD into a fixed one. Pull hard on the the trigger to retract it as far as possible and try to pull the piece straight out. This may seem obvious, but you wouldn't believe how often a novice has claimed a SLCD to be hopelessly stuck, only to have an expert remove it in a few seconds. If that doesn't work, look in the crack for an opening to move the unit through and carefully work the unit toward the edge of the crack. Clever and delicate maneuvering is the best bet for getting the unit free. Some climbers sling the triggers on their SLCDs, particularly the smaller ones, with cord to make removal easier if a unit should get stuck or if the trigger is inside the crack and cannot be reached. As a last resort, clip a sling to this cord with a carabiner and give it a good jerk. If the first tug or two doesn't free the piece, good luck!

Offset cams always should be avoided. This occurs when one cam is near minimum range, and another near maximum. It can happen in really wavy cracks, when the cams must adjust to extravagant differences in crack size. If such a placement is your only option, try a passive chock.

The Basic Essentials of Placing SLCDs

- Always align the unit with the stem pointing in the anticipated direction of pull.
- To keep the unit from "walking" because of rope drag during a lead, use a quickdraw to clip it off, unless the unit already features a sewn sling.
- Try to place the unit near the outside edge of the crack, where you can eyeball the cam lobes to determine their position. This way, you also can easily reach the trigger when time comes to clean the device.
- Strive for the ideal placement, with the cams 10 to 50 percent deployed in the most uniformly parallel section of the crack, so the cams cannot open if the unit walks a bit. Use a larger device over a smaller one, but, unless you are absolutely desperate, never force too big a unit into too small a hole. Once the cams are rolled to minimum width, removal, if possible, is dastardly.
- Never trust a placement where the cams are nearly "tipped," (the cam lobes almost fully deployed). In such a position, there is little room for further expansion, and stability is poor.
- Never place a rigid-stemmed unit so the stem is over a lip. A fall can either bend or break the unit.
- Take some time to fiddle with marginal placements on the ground. Clip a sling into the the SLCD and apply body weight to discover just how far you can trust it. But remember - body weight testing is far milder than a lead fall!

Offset cams also can occur in parallel-sided cracks. Remember, if you split the difference, the cams would be at 50 percent – or optimum range – so it's not a problem of size. Instead, the cams have been forced or wrenched into offsetting positions, which renders the placement worthless, or nearly so. When any cam is deployed beyond about eighty percent expansion, it only takes minimal movement for the cam to invert. So when the cams are either radically offset, inverted, or nearly inverted, the placement should be considered worthless.

Avoid "tipped-out" placements, where the cams are fully, or nearly fully, deployed. No camming device is capable of functioning correctly when the cams are at maximum expansion, except the Black Diamond Camalot. Other units

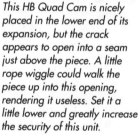

This HB Quad Cam is nicely placed in the lower end of its expansion, but the crack appears to open into a seam just above the piece. A little rope wiggle could walk the piece up into this opening, rendering it useless. Set it a little lower and greatly increase the security of this unit.

This HB Quad Cam is too small for the crack. It might work for aid in a pinch, but you'd be much better off using the next bigger size, or placing the piece higher, where the crack closes down a bit.

The cams on this Quad Cam are offset; by not loading the cams symmetrically, the stability of the piece is compromised. Always try to keep all cams at the same range of expansion.

are simply too small for these placements. A fall often will stress the unit just enough to make the cams invert, and the unit will blow out like an wind-blown umbrella, or the unit will walk to an opening in the crack and become utterly worthless.

For some reason, climbers often think the deeper you place a unit in the crack, the more secure it is. Not so. Your security is as good as the position of the cams and the relative soundness of the rock. When the unit is placed too deep, the trigger is hard to reach and the unit is that much harder to get out. Try to place the unit near the outside of the crack, or as near to that as placement allows. In soft desert sandstone, however, it's best to set the SLCD somewhat inside the crack, so an impact on the piece won't blow the edge of the crack out.

There is a lot of talk about the ability of camming units to swivel toward the direction of pull, once weighted. In most cases, this is true. The swiveling action will align the unit in the direction of the load, and also will align the cams for maximum strength and stability. But the fact is, you should avoid letting your protection swivel, because it may swivel right out of the crack, especially if the crack is wavy. Take special care to anticipate the direction of pull, and to align the unit accordingly when you place it. Basically, place the unit with the stem pointing in the anticipated direction of pull, and do whatever is necessary to ensure rope drag won't set the unit to walking inside the crack. Even nominal rope drag can change the unit's position, so most camming units nowadays come with sewn slings. Those that don't should be connected to the rope with a quickdraw when leading.

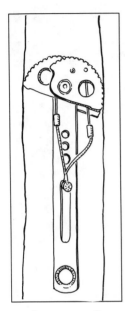

The cams are offset in this Friend. One side is tipped out. The Friend is just too small for the crack.

Today most SLCDs have sewn slings for connecting them to the rope with a carabiner. The sewn slings have less bulk than knotted clings, an dthey can't come accidentally untied. Inspect the slings regularly to make sure they are in good shape. A few companies, such as Yates Equipment, specialize in replacing the webbing on SLCDs. Knotted ⁄16-inch supertape or 5.5mm Spectra cord can also be used to sling a SLCD. With the supertape use a water knot, but keep your eyes on the tails because they will creep toward the knot. For Spectra cord the manufacturer recommends a triple fisherman's knot. Rigid Friends are intended to be slung in the large hole in the stem situated opposite of the cams. Some climbers sling their rigid Friends in the hole nearest the cams to reduce the leverage on the stem in shallow, horizontal cracks. Single cabled SLCDs usually have a sling hole at the end of the cable, and double cable SLCDs have a loop to tie into. Some SLCDs, notably Camalots, don't have a sling, so they should be fixed with a sling, or always be clipped into the rope with a quickdraw when leading.

Camming devices work in flaring cracks if the rock is sound and the flare is not so radical that the cam lobes cannot attain adequate bite. When a crack nears the critical flare angle, a fall loads the unit in an unstable manner. If the rock is poor as well, the placement can sheer out; even in dense granite, the unit can fail if the flare is too great.

With outward flaring cracks – where the lip of the crack is wider than the depths – you should jockey the unit around to find that spot where the difference in cam expansion is the least. If the rear cams are rolled tight, and the outside cams nearly tipped, you're looking at some pretty marginal pro. Though two cams actually can hold a fall, the unit tends to pivot when the other cams fail, and this pivoting can dislodge the unit altogether.

For tapering cracks – where the crack is wider below the placement – a couple of hours of tinkering with placements on the ground is advisable to fully understand where the critical taper angle starts.

All mechanical devices eventually become dirty. For optimal trigger and cam action, clean with soapy water and lubricate with a teflon or silicone lubricant. Elmer's Slide-All teflon lubricant is an excellent choice. Do not use oil or oil-based lubricants such as WD40, because they collect dirt, which will eventually gum up the cams, probably at the worst possible moment.

Camalots are the only camming device currently on the market with a double axle. The design means the Camalot can cover a significantly larger expansion range than other, comparably-sized devices. The added camming range is beneficial in flaring cracks, where the disparity of crack width is more pronounced, but comes at the price of increased weight. The Camalot works in the fully-deployed "umbrella" position as a passive nut, though it is somewhat unstable in this usage. The handle is a durable stainless steel cable. The trigger is a single-finger affair made of rugged Nylatron. The cams are stamped from 7075-T6 aluminum, and are narrower than those found on other SLCDs.

Whenever something is expensive and cherished, there is always someone out there pumping out cheap replicas. It's a safe bet that these knock offs will be inferior to the Real McCoy, even if they look the same. Some of the units look good enough, while others are clearly trash, with loose wires, poor action, wobbly cams, et al.

Before buying any SLCD, test the trigger action, and the smoothness with which the cams retract and expand. If the cams "wiggle" on the axle, the machining tolerances were not kept tight, which sacrifices the stability of the unit. Bear in mind the age-old saying, "You get what you pay for." In the case of SLCDs, or any climbing gear, buying cheap may land you in a maggot factory.

SLIDING NUTS

In brief, all sliding nuts work off the principle of opposing wedges. The first examples were simply two tapers arranged on one sling. Next came two cabled tapers, swaged together at the base to form a mutual clip-in loop. On one cable was a taper, right side up; on the other was another taper (of equal size), upside down, which could be moved up and down the cable. As the two tapers contacted each other, the width of the combined nut increased, eventually fitting the intended placement.

The original slider nuts are no longer on the market. Refinements in the original units – which were nearly impossible to remove from the rock – have left us the spring-loaded Cobras, Slugs and Lowe Balls, the only sliders now available. Expect to see other versions on the market soon, but don't hold your breath. Malcolm Daly of Trango USA has informed me that, in terms of manufacturing set-up, slider nuts are a hassle of the first order. In addition to the manufacturing hardships, slider nuts present some bewildering problems for both the reviewer and the consumer.

Both the Cobra and Lowe Ball work like magic, but you must know their limitations. First, slider nuts are small,

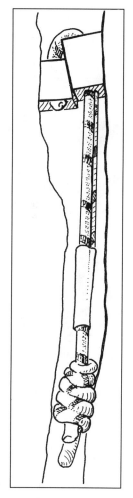

An original sliding nut pair was strung on one sling.

A Lowe Ball in a virtually perfect placement (one you will rarely get). Note that the symmetry of the crack matches both the fixed taper on the left, and the sliding half-ball component on the right. Likewise, notice that the sliding component is at mid-range on the fixed taper; the unit works best this way.

especially the smallest ones, which allow placement in the same size cracks as micro tapers. Even in ideal placements, the breaking strength is relatively low. Second, the placement is only as good as the purchase of either the cylinder or ball. Because the surface area contacting the rock is pretty small, the rock can break away if the unit is fallen on. Third, whenever the cylinder or ball is fully extended or at the end of its range, holding power is significantly reduced. Lastly, if the units are placed to hold large loads over sharp edges (a use for which they were not designed), they might hold, but the impact will invariably kink the cable and you'll have to retire them.

A taper has obvious advantages over the more elaborate slider nuts in most placements. Most likely, you'll find stoppers are stronger, more straightforward to place and remove, and get more surface area on the stone. But in thin, shallow, parallel-sided cracks – and plenty exist – slider nuts often provide the only option for protection. If you place one on lead, try to place two and equalize them, or use a Yates Screamer.

SUMMARY

Selecting your purchase from such a panoply of available protection can be as confusing as buying a new car. It becomes all the more baffling when you read the "information" provided in product catalogues. Most manufacturers are guilty of overstating their product's capabilities – just the standard business of promotion. We should remember this: The rock-climbing market, though steadily growing, still is small and limited. Any product has to be viable or it simply won't last. Almost without exception, all the devices listed herein are first-rate in terms of design and construction. Selection, then, can best be decided by determining the climbing situations you will most likely encounter, and knowing what gear is specifically suited for it.

Tapers and camming devices have several standard types, and as the sport evolves, so does the archetypal design. The archetype represents the nut that is best suited for generic use in the United States. When you move too far away from the archetype, you gain advantage in specialized situations at the loss (though limited, mind you) of overall utility. With tapers, the standard used to be the straight taper, but now the curved taper is the archetype. A majority of American climbing is done on granite, sandstone, or rock that fractures in a similar manner, with reasonably uniform cracks. Hence, your basic curved taper probably is best for general use. Not so in conglomerate rock, where your cutaway or scooped tapers can snag on crystals inside a crack.

The four-cam, solid-stem unit is the archetypal camming device. When you move to the three-cam units, you gain the advantage of lower profile, but one less cam means less surface area on the rock and a reduction, however small, in security.

The point is, all the under-designed gear lacks specific features, and is a little better suited as a generic tool. If much of your climbing is done on rock requiring odd-tailored gear, that's what you should buy. Active local climbers are the best instructors in what gear works best at a given crag. Remember that with the exception of offset tapers, which definitely under-perform a regular taper in parallel-sided cracks, most of the other gear can function almost equally well in a given situation, provided the gear is used by someone who understands its nuances. Fact is, the difference gear makes in your climbing usually is overstated. If you can get one brand of nut to fit, other brands will probably work just as well. That assumes, of course, that the nut is either American or British-made. American and British products are, by any engineering or manufacturing standards, far superior to all others.

In talking with various manufacturers, I have realized just how unique the rock gear business is. Not one of the manufacturers sets the top priority on making money (which seems so remarkable that I'm not certain I believe it). Their stated aim is to produce a great product. The understanding, it would seem, is that a good product will result in good profits. All talked with deserved pride about their products. A hell of a lot of care, passion and engineering creativity is evident in modern rock-climbing hardware, and every climber is indebted to these manufacturers because each has taken our needs so seriously.

There is remarkable parity amongst all the gear competing for your greenback. Ultimately, it's not the gear, but the person placing it that makes the difference. Considering that 30 years ago, British climbers used to protect their most difficult leads with machine nuts found on the railroad tracks, the present-day climber should appreciate having such wide choices among what 90 percent of the time is fabulous gear.

This HB Cobra makes good contact with the rock, but is situated so near to the edge that a little rope wiggle could dislodge it. It also appears that if the rock is less than perfectly solid, the right edge of the crack could crumble away.

NUT TOOLS

Nut tools come in a variety of shapes and styles. All the good ones feature a hook-shaped end that is capable of pushing, pulling and otherwise prodding a stubborn nut loose, plus a hole for tying a keeper cord. A nut tool will more than pay for itself by helping you avoid loosing stubborn gear, and should be a standard item on every rack. Even more specialized are tools designed to remove unyielding SLCDs. This item may be more extra gear than you need to carry, unless you seem to have a persistent problem with stuck SLCDs.

Fixed Gear

I recall the time British ace Ron Fawcett and I were trying to speed climb the South Face of Washington Column in Yosemite. Up in the middle is a left-slanting arch, which at that time bristled with fixed gear. Presuming the gear was all bomber, I never tested anything, or even looked at it; I simply started clipping across it. About fifteen feet off the belay, a fixed nut popped the second I weighted it; Ron was inattentive, dropped me about forty feet and I wrenched to a stop as close as my next breath to a chopper flake, all the hide raked off my knuckles.

As this tale shows, there is only one rule of thumb to remember about fixed gear: never trust it outright. One summer, a new fixed pin might be so bomber that Herman Munster couldn't clean it with an eight-pound sledge. But after the winter's freeze and thaw, that same pin may be as loose as a tent stake in peat. Fixed nuts tend to be more reliable, but not always. Remember two things: Somebody probably has tried like hell to clean the nut, and it's position has probably been changed. Because it's fixed doesn't mean it will hold a fall, only that it's stuck. Always check the placement. Since everybody and his brother has tried to clean it, the cable is probably damaged. Fixed micros are almost always abused and worthless. Same goes for SLCDs. Various cleaning widgets and the dread of leaving a $50 device behind makes fixed SLCDs a rare, but not unseen, occurrence. Usually, the cams are rolled so tight you'd need a hacksaw to get the unit out. Still, consider the unit unreliable. The maxim is: Eyeball and test any and all fixed anchors, and presume they are suspect even if they look good. And back them up whenever possible.

PITONS

While pitons no longer have much practical value in free climbing, they are absolutely essential for big walls. Knowledge of their use, however, is essential to appreciating their limits as fixed anchors.

Pitoncraft is best left up to the individual to develop, but several things are worth mentioning. First, common sense is the rule. You want to use a piton that fits the crack and enters about 75 percent of the way in before you start hammering on it. Both the spine and the two running edges of the peg should have good bite in the crack, and the peg should ring as you drive it home. Try to bury it to the hilt, but don't overdrive it, or you'll either never get it out, or ruin it trying to. In soft rock, particularly desert sandstone, you can almost create your own placement by blasting an oversized pin into an undersized crack. But it still might

(Opposite Page)
Mary Suvela climbs
fixed bolts on Shipoopi!
(5.12a) in Tuolumne
Meadows.

photo: Chris Falkenstein

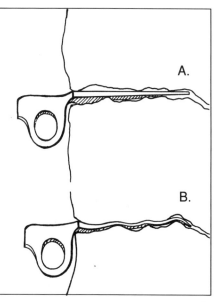

A.

B.

Hard steel pitons (A.)
blast their way into a
crack, chiseling a tight
fit. Soft steel pitons (B.)
are still found fixed on
many older routes, and
work by conforming
tightly with the
undulations of the crack.
Both types of pitons will
loosen with weathering
and time.

come out with your fingers. Piton use in any rock creates such a vile scar that you want to use nuts whenever possible.

The best way to learn pitoncraft is to grab a handful of pegs, a hammer and aid slings, go to some junky crag where nobody climbs, and experiment low to the ground. Bang in a few, and stand on them to see just how much or how little various placements will hold. After dinking around for a couple of hours, you'll get the hang of it. Since pitons are virtually never used to protect free climbing anymore, the best way to get dialed in is to venture onto a beginning wall climb – a "trade route" like Yosemite's Leaning Tower or the Dihedral Wall. Once you get to the top, you'll have it down pat.

Assuming you have no interest in big walls, have no hammer as you approach a fixed piton belay station, or must rely on fixed pins for lead protection, how do you gauge the security of your anchor? First, inspect the pins. How rusty are they? Do they move? Are they fully driven, or do they hang halfway out of the crack? Are they wee and creaky knifebades, funky soft steel European pegs, or beafy Lost Arrows or Angles? As with tapers, the bigger the better. Do they cam into a hole in the crack, or will a hard pull likely twist them from their placement? At best, it's still a crap shoot, so back up fixed pins whenever possible.

I can say it, but many climbers still won't believe that a piece of iron beat into a crack is not necessarily sound. To prove my point, we've got to go back to Suicide Rock in the early 70s. The name was never more germane than for a young climber from the San Diego area known affectionately as "Acapulco Bill," a moniker he "earned" after a string of spectacular falls that more resembled cliff diving than leader falls. Since Acapulco Bill would only lead, he fell often and far, so far that he had no right to continue on this earth. Somehow, he got it in his mind that every fixed pin was solid as Excalibur in situ. Whenever he would spot a fixed pin, he'd slot a quick nut and rush headlong, often running the rope out upwards of fifty feet in his mad quest for some cracked and rusty peg hammered home by John Mendenhall in the thirties. Twice, I saw him lunge for such a peg; twice, I saw the peg ping out in his hands; and twice I saw Acapulco Bill pitch off for one of his legendary dives. I think it was his wife who finally got him back to the beach and away from the crags.

Anyway, there are four basic piton designs. Knifeblades (called Bugaboos in the larger sizes) come in six sizes, from ⅛ to ³⁄₁₆ inch in width, and from 3 to 4⅞ inches in length. Precision grinding ensures a constant taper. Lost Arrows (a.k.a. horizontals) come in eight sizes, from ⁵⁄₃₂ to ⁹⁄₃₂ inch in width, and from 1¾ to 4⅝ inches long. Angles come in six sizes, from ½ to 1½ inches. The RURP (Realized Ultimate Reality Piton), a postage stamp-sized peg with a thin, half-inch long blade, is for aid only.

The designs have changed little in 20 years. The hot-forging method is age-old and unsurpassed, and the 4130 chrome-moly steel is harder than rock. European imports generally are inferior. All told, Black Diamond pitons probably are the best mass-produced line in the world.

BOLTS

For more than 50 years, the bolt was the bane of sportsmanlike climbing, though it always played an important role. First ascensionists justified the judicious bolt, but routinely risked great peril to avoid placing them. For better or worse, the attitudes of sport climbing have changed all that, and presently, the majority of the most notorious routes are predominantly, if not entirely, bolt-protected. The bold runout is, for the most part, a thing of the past. Since bolts now play such a leading role in current climbing – at all levels – it's best we go into some detail about them.

The majority of bolts placed on current routes are ⅜ or ½ inch in diameter, and were designed as concrete anchors for industrial use. Though not specifically designed for use in rock climbing, the specs are sufficient to warrant their use as rock climbing anchors. When properly fitted, they are remarkably strong, and should remain so for many years. The same cannot be said of the ¼-inch diameter bolts placed at some areas as late as the mid-eighties; and since so many of these bolts have not yet been replaced by newer bolts, it behooves us to see what we're up against. But first, let's examine bolting in general.

Consider the hole. This used to be tunneled out by hammering on a "shank rotary drill" rig – basically a drill held in a rolled steel holder. By hammering on the holder and twisting it at the same time, the hole is laboriously drilled. In those days, it took up to a half hour to bore a 1½ inch deep hole in granite – even longer in dense limestone. For decades, this tedious labor deterred excessive bolting, but the introduction of lightweight battery-fed electric drills, and, more recently, gas-powered drills (principally the Bosch Bulldog), has changed all that. Now, it takes thirty seconds to drill a hole.

The actual bolt is nail-like, and may be one of several types: The contraction bolt, which has a split shaft that is compressed as it is driven into the hole; and the expansion bolt, which expands an attached steel sleeve when tightened with a wrench, or as it is driven in. Glue-in bolts have seen limited use in the United States, which is probably good because they must be set with great care to be sure the glue adheres properly.

Once set, carabiners can be clipped into the bolt hanger, a strip of bent metal that usually is secured via a nut screwed into the bolt. Some bolts feature hangers already affixed to

the bolt before it is driven home. Most of the new ⅜ and ½ inch bolts have a minimum strength of over 4,000 pounds, if properly placed in solid rock. The older, ¼ inch bolts are not nearly so strong, and lose strength significantly after several seasons in the rock.

I purposefully have neglected the business of how to place bolts. Establishing routes that require bolts traditionally has been and should remain in the realm of the expert, and therefore is beyond the scope of this book. If you do place bolts, make sure you take the time to learn their proper use, as the lives of others will ride on your craftsmanship. More than one person has hit the deck because of another's sloppy work.

Bolt History

Through the fifties, sixties and seventies, Rawl Drive bolts were the norm. These bolts were wedge-type hammer-ins, and can still be found on classic climbs in Yosemite, Tahquitz, the Tetons and a host of other areas. A variety of oddball bolts – usually whatever was available at the local hardware store – also were used in various desert areas, but many times these bolts were so inferior that climbers chose instead to bang a ½ inch baby angle piton into a ⅜ inch drilled hole. Anyway, for 20 years, the bolt of choice was the old Rawl Drive, which consisted of a ¼ or ⅜ inch sleeve/stud with a tip machined like a drill bit. The actual bolt stud was used as the drill. After the hole was drilled, a conical wedge was fitted into the hollow-ended stud, which in turn was hammered home. When the conical wedge hit the back of the hole, it expanded the stud and secured the bolt. Another type of Rawl Drive bolt used an independent drill for the hole. Initially, these bolts were strong enough, provided the hole was drilled to an exact depth. Too shallow and the stud hung too far out of the hole; too deep and the wedge would not expand the sleeve. You can still see these bolts, or ones like them, on the Steck/Salathe on Sentinel, the Nose of El Capitan and the Lost Arrow Spire.

In about 1965, most climbers changed over to the Rawl Drive contraction-type hammer-in bolt. These ¼ inch hammer-ins featured a split shank that was squeezed together when banged into the narrow hole. The outward spring force against the walls of the hole kept the bolt snug – for a while. These bolts came in both buttonhead and screw-top styles, the latter being the weaker because of its threads. For nearly 20 years, these contraction bolts were used without question, and were employed easily five to one over all other designs. Only after about 10 years did their real shortcomings come to light.

The two bolts on the left are to be feared and loathed: The top left is a quarter-inch diameter buttonhead compression bolt; the lower left bolt is a quarter-inch Rawl stud expansion bolt. These types of bolts have broken at loads as low as 1000 pounds (during testing), which is insufficient to hold a hard leader fall. The bolts on the right represent the modern standard: The upper right is a half-inch Rawl 5-piece, which has a whopping 10,000 pounds shear strength; the lower right is a three-eighths-inch Rawl stud, which has a shear strength of about 5,400 pounds.

First, contraction bolts are under constant pressure. Given time, that pressure decreases and the bolt's outward-spring force becomes far less; thus, the bolt can creep from the hole as the tension relaxes. Radical changes in temperatures – sweltering summers and freezing winters – hasten the process. Second, the metal is prone to corrosion, the rate of corrosion being tied to the mineral content of the rock. Bolts rust horribly, in other words. Improper placement, crooked or oblique holes, weakening through hammer blows and a slew of other problems, make even a perfectly set ¼ inch contraction bolt a liability after only a few seasons. Lastly, it takes considerable resistance to fully depress the bolt's split shank, something impossible in softer rock like sandstone or quartz monzonite. More often than not, Rawl Drive bolts placed in soft rock deform the hole and never accomplish the requisite outward-spring tension needed to make them even remotely adequate as an anchor. Consequently, you should not trust a ¼ inch contraction bolt in softer rock, even if it's been placed recently.

Why more of these ¼ inch contraction bolts have not failed is one of climbing's great mysteries. But just how poor many of them had become was never better illustrated than when several local Suicide and Tahquitz climbers set to replace all the old bolts in the Idyllwild climbing areas. Recall that before the sticky boot revolution of the early '80s, the harder climbs at Suicide were much sought after, and many teams spent whole afternoons "falling up" them. Yet bolts that had held literally thousands of falls often were removed with a single hammer blow! The message here is that extreme care should be used before trusting old contraction bolts. Though they were strong enough initially, time has drastically reduced their strength. This type of bolt was designed not for rock climbing, but as lightweight industrial anchors for concrete and masonry, and they usually had served their intended purpose after a few weeks or months. They were never intended to act as the point from which a person's life could hang, nor for decades of such use. If you do have to clip a sketchy ¼ inch bolt for lead pro, use a Screamer, back it up if possible, and don't fall.

Even worse than ¼ inch bolts are ¼ inch bolts with no hangers. Doubtless some blockhead pilfered the hanger, and left you at the headwaters of Shit Creek. If you must climb this route (as opposed to going down, which should always be an option if the anchors are bogus), the best trick is to slide the head down on a smaller-sized wired taper, slip the newly exposed loop of cable over the stud, and cinch the head tight against the stud. Hopefully, the stud still has a nut to hold the taper cable on, otherwise the placement is good only for aid. Even with a nut, this dicey connection to the bolt will not hold any outward pull, so don't fall!

There was a scandal a few years back when some distributors from hell were counterfeiting inferior bolts made from low-grade materials instead of the stronger alloys specified for anchors. It is not inconceivable that this type of alarming profiteering still occurs on occasion. While modern bolts have taken tons (literally) of abuse with few mishaps, no single anchor, bolt or chock should be considered 100% reliable. Backups are essential, especially for belay and rappel anchors. Among the most dangerous times of a lead are the beginning of a pitch or just above a ledge, where few bolts or chocks separate the leader from the ground or ledge. To make matters worse, the impact force a leader can generate is greatest early in the pitch, when only a small amount of rope is available to absorb the shock of the fall.

In the early eighties, when climbers first started using something other than Rawl contraction bolts, the USE Diamond Taper ¼ inch bolt gained momentary popularity. The required ¼ inch hole was routine to drill, and the Diamond Taper Bolt tested out okay. This push-type bolt is installed by screwing the tapered, threaded section into a lead sleeve, expanding the sleeve outward. Installation is straightforward, but the Taper Bolt is very tricky to place correctly. Inserting and hammering on the bolt easily mauls the lead sleeve. The gap between the head of the bolt and the rock must be judged exactly prior to torquing, because a specific number of turns is required for full strength. One turn too few seriously decreases its holding power, and one turn too many can strip the lead sleeve, rendering the bolt useless. Even climbers experienced with the Taper Bolt often botched placement, and worse yet, a poorly placed Taper Bolt is hard to detect without a crow bar. Consequently – and thankfully – the Taper Bolt has fallen out of favor, is not recommended, and should be used with extreme caution when found on a route.

Glue-in bolts are popular in Europe and are not unheard of in the United States. One system for placing them is to hammer a ⅜ inch, coarse-threaded machine bolt into a drilled hole filled with polyester resin. (Beware of epoxy, which can corrode the bolt.) These bolts are strong enough (the resin is often stronger than the rock), but everything has to be placed perfectly. An oversized hole – even by a few thousandths of an inch – makes the bolt useless. Certain materials (grade 2 steel) are too weak, others (grade 8 steel) too hard for the threads to achieve adequate bite in the hole. And the practice is not sound in anything but the hardest rock. In almost all instances, the glue-in is far inferior to other bolts.

Modern sport-climbing routes do not feature the old-style Rawl Drive bolts, glue-in bolts, or any bolt of ¼ inch diameter. The modern standard calls for expansion bolts of ⅜ to ½ inch in diameter. The Rawl "5-piece" and Rawl stud are the most popular bolts on the United States scene today.

The Rawl 5-piece is a "pull-out"-type bolt that pulls a cone into an expanding sleeve by cranking on the bolt head with a wrench. The Rawl 5-piece is one of the best rock bolts available. It has good strength (7,900 pounds sheer strength for the ⅜ inch), is suitable for a variety of rock surfaces and is relatively foolproof to install. For full-strength protection, the Rawl bolt is torqued until the blue plastic sleeve starts to compress, which is apparent when the torquing force becomes constant (usually after three or four turns). Modest cost, availability, straightforward installation and general reliability has made the Rawl 5-piece the bolt of choice.

The Rawl stud also pulls a cone into an expanding sleeve, but in this case only when a nut is tightened on the threaded bolt. While not quite as strong as the Rawl 5-piece because of the threads on the bolt, the Rawl stud is quicker and easier to place for those few remaining mavericks who do their bolting on the lead.

Metolius has developed a new generation of bolt – the "S.S." – designed to couple with their "S.S." (stainless steel) hanger. A basic "expansion-type" bolt, the "S.S." is a straight-shafted, stainless steel bolt with a knurled expansion sleeve. The cone nut is brass. The "S.S." is specifically designed for climbing, and the materials and design most likely make the "S.S." the most bomber bolt on the market. A special half-inch size is suitable for soft rock (shear and pullout strength an astronomical 7,000 lbs.); the ⅜ incher is for hard rock (shear and pullout strength – 5,000 lbs). However, the high cost of these have limited their use.

Bolt Hangers

With the rise in popularity of sport climbing has come a slew of new bolt hanger designs, ranging from primitive homemade jobs to slick, strong commercial hangers. Any of the commercially available hangers are certain to meet the specs required for the situation, but homemade hangers may or may not. Aluminum hangers, homemade or otherwise, should be considered suspect if they have taken repeated high-force falls. Always eyeball suspect hangers for cracks or other deformation.Titanium or stainless steel are the materials of choice. Metolius has led the current trend to minimize the visual impact of fixed anchors by offering three colors of camouflaged stainless steel hangers. If not using these, responsible first ascensionists are painting their hangers to match the color of the rock. A highly corrosion resistant, strong and super light Russian titanium hanger has recently been brought into the country by Trango USA. Petzl, Blue Water and SMC also make good hangers, along with a handful of other companies I have missed.

Homemade hangers run the gamut from sawed off and drilled angle iron to double links of chain. As mentioned above, some are good, some are bad– it's your guess. Some of the older homemades, nicknamed "pop-offs," feature a design that twists the downward pull of a falling climber into an outward pull on the bolt stud, which could prove disastrous with an old ¼ inch contraction bolt. Beware of any hanger that levers the bolt outward.

A trend at some sport-climbing areas for the past few years has been to use construction cold shuts (hooks) for hangers – either open, closed or welded. The advantage of cold shuts is their relatively large diameter and rounded surface, which allows the rope to be placed directly through the hanger for lowering. Two open cold shuts are fixed at the tops of many routes, so when you finish the climb, you simply drape the rope through the open shuts and lower off. Though the people who set them swear by them, others are leery to toprope off such hangers. Closed cold shuts may be adequate for lowering and toproping situations, but are not up to snuff for lead protection.

What to do with that bolt . . .

There is no absolutely reliable method to test in situ bolts, but there are plenty of reasons to want to. Here are some suggestions:

- Always consider a ¼ inch bolt suspect. They are no longer placed as anchors, though they are commonly found on older routes.
- Make sure the bolt hanger is flush to the wall and not a "spinner," where the hanger spins freely on the stud. A spinner indicates the hole was drilled too shallow for the bolt stud, or that the bolt stud has crept out from the hole, which happens with contraction bolts. And don't try to "fix" the spinner by hammering on it. Had that been possible, the first party would have sunk it. Further hammering can only damage the shank and the head.
- Keep an eye out for "cratering," which occurs in brittle or extremely hard rock, and is usually the result of sloppy drilling, which forms a chipped-away crater around the hole. Cratering can greatly reduce the bolt's purchase because the rock surrounding the shank is damaged.
- Check the hanger for cracks.
- If the bolt is a "screw-head," make sure the nut is snug and the threads are in good shape. I learned this after taking a thirty-foot grounder (into a snow bank, luckily) when the hanger popped off the denuded threads of such a bolt. If the bolt is a "buttonhead," or looks like a machine bolt, again make sure it's snugly set and free of fatigue cracks.
- If the bolt is clearly bent, or looks to be set in an oblique hole, beware! Discoloration is natural enough, but excessive rust denotes a "coffin nail."

Use common sense. If the bolt looks funky, don't trust it. And always back up bolts (that don't meet the modern standard) with a nut, if possible. A perfect bolt is nearly impossible to pull out, even with an astronomical fall, but there are a lot of bolts out there that are something less than perfect. Better safe than splattered.

Welded cold shuts have been available that meets the standard for lead climbing, lowering and toproping. Reportedly, it's slightly easier for a quickdraw to accidentally unclip from a welded cold shut than from a traditional hanger, but the cold shut offers easy retreat from any point on the route and is easier on carabiners.

WEBBING

One of my first climbing outings was to Suicide Rock in Idyllwild, California – in winter. Rick Accomazzo and I spent two hours post-holing through hip-deep snow drifts just getting to the crag, which had a thirty-foot snow cone at its base – a boon, we reckoned, since the top of the cone put us above the crux lower moves of several then-prestigious routes. Ricky roped up, front-pointed up the snow cone and went to work on "Frustration." He got about ten feet up a hinging lieback and set a nut, his wet boots skedaddling all over the place. Two moves higher, he popped, the one-inch sling on the nut broke, and Ricky, poor fellow, slammed into and through the crust of the hollow snow cone, leaving behind a perfect sketch of his body, the kind detectives scribble around a slain thug on the tarmac. By the time Ricky had clawed his way out of the hole, his fingers were so numb that for two weeks afterwards he had to use his thumbs to take a leak. Our mistake was to string a nut with a sling we'd filched off a rappel anchor out at Joshua Tree. Who knows how old it was, or how it had been abused. Never again.

Slings that are 1, ⅝ and ⁹⁄₁₆ inch in width are routinely used to anchor setups, as tie-ins, for equalizing two or more separate anchors, and for connecting ropes to trees, flakes, tunnels and other natural rock features. For this reason, let's take a brief look at available materials.

Since World War II, nylon webbing has been widely used in rock climbing. Invented to batten down gear on P.T. boats, climbers have found nylon webbing (flat rope, or "tape") useful as gear slings, runners and tie-offs. Later, several wraps of the one or two-inch variety came to form the "swami belt," the standard tie-in device (a harness of sorts) for more than 20 years. As of about 1980, formal harnesses – feather light and heroically strong – have virtually replaced the old swami belts, and webbing presently is used almost exclusively as sling material.

For 45 years, standard nylon webbing was used exclusively to form slings of 1 and ⁹⁄₁₆ inch diameter, the latter for tying off pitons. Five-eighths-inch sling was introduced about 15 years ago. The strength of the material was more than adequate for its applications. The shortcomings of pure nylon, however, are that it weakens with age and use, and as is the case with all webbing, it is adversely affected by exposure to sunlight's ultraviolet rays.

The great majority of nylon webbing is manufactured for the military, and the government has set minimum requirements, or "specs," that the webbing must meet for use in life-support situations. "Mil-spec" simply refers to these government, or military specifications. Blue Water has gone several steps further than the minimum mil-specs to produce their Climb-Spec webbing.

The standard mil-spec webbing has a corduroy-type finish because of the many small ridges in the weave. Climb-Spec has refined this weave, eliminating the ridges to produce a "sateen" finish, which is essentially flat and smooth to the touch. This new weave affords two significant advantages: First, it allows a greater density of nylon thread, increasing the strength (of one-inch webbing) some 500 pounds; second, and more importantly, it increases the wear-resistance upwards of 50 percent. Blue Water Climb-Spec is available in both 1 and $\frac{9}{16}$ inch, and comes in bulk form or pre-sewn runners. The 1 inch sling tests out at 7,400 pounds (some 2,000 lbs. higher than standard webbing), while the $\frac{9}{16}$ inch is good to 4,500 lbs.

Though nylon is still a viable material for slings, other far superior materials have come to replace it for the most part. Blue Water's Spectra is a remarkable material, a molecular-weight polyethylene developed by Allied-Signal Inc. It is the strongest fiber ever made. Pound-for-pound, it is ten times stronger than steel. It is also about ten times as expensive. Spectra-sewn runners are available only in $\frac{9}{16}$ inch (in various lengths), and are for those who want half the bulk and weight of other runners with no significant reduction in strength. According to Bill Griggers of Blue Water, the company doesn't manufacture 1-inch Spectra slings because the cost would be prohibitive and a 12,000-pound test webbing is absurd overkill. Spectra's wear resistance is excellent. When cut, Spectra will not tear through. And because it tests out at 6,000-plus lbs. and is very supple and workable for knots, Spectra has become the sling of choice throughout the United States.

Aside from the price, Spectra does have some minor shortcomings, however. It is 19 percent less resistant to damage caused by sunlight than regular mil-spec nylon, and it is too slick to work as well as nylon for the friction knots used in self-rescue situations (prusik knot, Klemheist, etc.). In addition, it should be tied into a loop using a bulky triple grapevine, and it has a low melting temperature, so it can be burned easily by a rope running across it.

Without question, these new fibers are superior to standard mil-spec nylon for use as sling material. That is not to say that mil-spec runners are no good, however. There have been isolated cases of mil-spec runners tearing over razor-sharp edges. And nylon does wear out, so it is not unheard of for old runners to break under the impact of a fall. But I have never heard of a sling in good condition breaking when the system has been properly rigged. Consequently, the less-expensive mil-spec webbing continues to be a viable choice for slings, provided the climber keeps a sharp eye on its condition, and retires it when signs of wear are obvious. As mentioned, exposure to sunlight greatly reduces the webbing's strength. If the nylon feels stiff, it probably has been affected by sunlight – but the webbing may be weakened and show no such sign. If there is any doubt, retire your runners after using them for a period of, say, a hundred days, remembering that the relatively inexpensive nylon is far less precious than your life.

Sewn webbing loops are stronger, lighter and less bulky than knotted ones, so most climbers these days use sewn slings for the most part. Slings equipped with a water knot can come in handy for tying around trees, flakes and tunnels in the event of a retreat, but you should check the water knots frequently, as they have a tendancy to come untied.

Short, sewn loops of webbing called quickdraws are one of the principle uses of webbing these days. Quickdraws are mandatory equipment for clipping the lead rope into bolts and chocks; they prevent rope drag and decrease the liklihood that the rope will wiggle a chock out of its placement.

CORDAGE

Nuts in larger sizes often are machined to accept 5.5MM cordage. What cordage to use is easy to determine, as there are only two kinds made specifically for this use: Spectra, by Blue Water, and Gemini (a Spectra/Kevlar blend), by Black Diamond. Both are very resistant to abrasion, and so strong they will never break, provided they have not been used beyond their lifespan of about a hundred field days. After that, stiffness and strength reduction due to ultraviolet exposure dictates you replace the cord. Perlon cord also will suffice as chock cord, though it is not nearly as strong, and is less wear-resistant.

PART TWO:

Complex Anchors

Complex anchors consist of multiple anchor components connected together to provide redundant and multi-directional belay anchors, toprope anchors, rappel anchors and bivouac anchors.

If no substantial natural anchor – a tree, block, or large bush – is available on your chosen climb, you must construct an artificial anchor using nuts. Given that you understand how to place nuts, the trick becomes how to connect them together to create a viable anchor system. Constructing a multi-nut anchor will at first take some time and trouble, but a trained eye and the knack for finding propitious nut slots – both a result of experience – quickly make this routine. Climbers are called on to do this many times each outing, so the training comes quickly.

If you only learn one thing from this book, let it be the Golden Rule: An anchor system is not adequate unless it can withstand the greatest force that can possibly be put to it. This is common sense, plain and simple. The fact that there are comparatively few instances of outright belay, toprope or rappel anchor failures suggests that climbers are particularly observant of the golden rule. However, anchors do fail, and tragedy usually follows.

This would be an ideal place for a ghastly account of anchor failure, but there's no need to get into the business of death here. If you're keen on the subject, thumb through any number of annual journals about accidents in American climbing and you'll see that few survive a total anchor failure – all the more reason to read closely, and make sure it never happens to you.

Before we get into specifics, let's go over some general concepts concerning what not to do. First, never belay from one anchor point unless it's a tree the size of the Washington Monument, or a block bigger than your garage. Even so, redundancy is safety. However, if you climb long enough, you're bound to run into a situation where you have to belay from a single anchor – perhaps a poor one. Allow me an anecdote here to show you just how dreadful it can be.

The Shield is neither the grimmest or the longest aid route on El Capitan, but toward the top of that vast, overhanging curtain of orange granite, the exposure is strictly world-class. At the end of one of those long RURP-and-blade pitches, I hit a rivet ladder and finally the belay – a hanging one, of course, from one sorry, rusted, mushroomed, buttonhead bolt. Without a hanger. This was in the mid-seventies, before the route had seen many ascents and obviously before anyone had bolstered the anchors. Anyway, the haulbag, Mike Lechlinski and I found ourselves hanging on that single, miserable bolt. The rivet ladder above looked bleak, more so because the previous ascent party had tied off every rivet with hero loops that had somehow cinched so tight we couldn't get them off without a knife – which, of course, we didn't have. Over the winter, the loops had bleached and frayed, and now they flapped in the wind like little threads of gauze. As Mike took off, holding his breath on every frazzled loop, on every creaking rivet, I tried to study the river below, or watch cars creep along the loop road, but every few seconds my eyes would snap back to that sorry bolt. I saw it rotate in the hole. I heard it creak, then snap like a toothpick. Twice, I saw it melt out of the hole. I put my thumb over it, both thumbs over it. I imagined a loop snapping on one of those rivets, and Mike zippering down onto that jive bolt, which surely would pop, and I wept pitifully and pissed my pants. I made a quick and binding pact with our Savior that if I ever got off that stinking rock alive, I'd devote my life to the poor and bereft. It was a horrible experience.

Next consideration: Never trust a fixed anchor setup outright, no matter how bombproof it appears. Many things can disguise just how poor an anchor may be, particularly a huge knot of slings from previous parties who obviously trusted the thing. Why shouldn't you? Consider the big stump that used to be atop Arch Rock in Yosemite. There was no less than fifty runners slung around it; thousands of climbers had belayed and rappeled off it for a dozen years. Richard Harrison took the time to check it one day and found that it was loose. We got behind it and pushed with our legs and the thing popped from the dirt like a mushroom and pitched off the cliff, nearly killing a team of Colorado climbers below. It was ready to go, and had been for God knows how long.

The point is: Fifty slings don't prove that an anchor isn't garbage. Don't be deceived by an anchor that appears sound, no matter the evidence that other climbers have long trusted it. I could go on and on about what to look for with fixed anchors, but the bottom line will always hinge on two points: Are the component anchor points (be they bolts, fixed pins, nuts, or a mix) sound, and if so, are they tied off in a way that is likewise sound. Examine the anchor and understand why it is good (or bad) *before* you trust it.

When no fixed anchors exist, you must set your own. In doing so, always consider the following details:

- Find a spot that provides convenient anchor placements. Take a moment to plan the entire system. Analyze the situation and prepare the anchors for any possible direction of pull.
- Keep the system simple, so it is quick to set and easy to double-check and keep tabs on. Use the minimal amount of gear to safely and efficiently do the job, which is usually

three or four bombproof anchors, and more if they are less than bombproof.

- As mentioned, remember that any anchor is only as strong as the rock it is set in.
- Make sure the anchor system is Solid, Redundant, Equalized, and allows No Extension, or SRENE. (This acronym is somewhat modified from one used by the American Mountain Guides Association.)

This all can sound overly technical and complicated, but in fact all of these concepts are based on common sense and simple mechanical laws that are usually self evident once you gain experience. Still, let us look closer at the fundemental concepts behind SRENE:

SRENE Anchors:
Solid
Redundant
Equalizated
No Extension

Solid means just that. The individual anchors and the system as a whole must be bombproof, able to stop a rogue elephant, without question.

Redundancy generally means placing three or four solid anchors (more if the anchors are less than ideal). Never use only one nut. Never. Most experienced climbers don't consider an anchor secure until they have set a minimum of three good nuts. Two bombproof anchors is the absolute minimum. In emergencies, climbers occasionally will use a single bolt, tree, or tied-off boulder for an anchor, but secure backup anchors will greatly reduce the chance of a catastrophe. Redundancy should exist through the entire anchor system: all anchors, slings and carabiners should be backed up. Redundancy also can include setting anchors in more than one crack system, to avoid relying on a single rock feature.

Equalization distributes the load equally between the various anchors in the system, to increase the overall strength of the system and to reduce the chance of a single anchor pulling out under stress.

No extension means that if one of the anchors in the system should fail, the system will not suddenly become slack and drop the climber a short distance, shock-loading the remaining anchors.

I'll say it again: We don't tie into an anchor with only one carabiner because we don't want to trust our lives to one piece of gear. For the same reason, we never trust one nut, piton, or bolt as a belay anchor because there is no back up. And backing up the system, or "system redundancy," is the key to staying alive. Certainly, we can trust a single block the size and girth of the Great Pyramid, but little less. Since it is so infrequent that we can get such a block, most anchors are matrixes – combinations of various nut configurations. More on this later.

*Dale Bard comes up on
a dicey anchor 2,000
feet up El Capitan.*

photo: Dave Diegelman

Knots for Anchoring

Knots play an essential role in creating anchor systems and tying into them. A handful of knots will cover the job nicely, so there's no need to get into gordian knots and others so complicated they would flummox the Ancient Mariner. (Let it be known that Jim Bridwell, one of the most experienced climbers in the history of the sport, uses only four knots for any and all climbing situations). Better to learn a few knots well, than a multitude of knots poorly.

Ring Bend

Also known as the water knot, the ring bend is used to tie sections of webbing into slings. Check the ring bend every time you use the sling to make sure the tails are at least three inches long, as slippery nylon has a penchant for creeping and untying itself.

Double Fisherman's

The double fisherman's, or Grapevine knot is a much more secure but bulky knot for tying slings together. This knot is also used to tie two rappel ropes together and to tie cordage

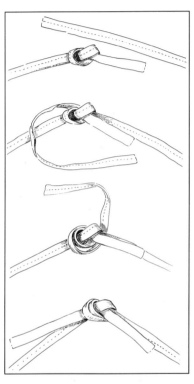

The Ring Bend (above), and the Double Fisherman's knot (left).

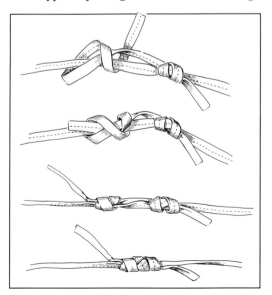

into slings. A double fisherman's in webbing creeps much more slowly than a ring bend, but still it should be checked periodically to make sure the tails are sufficiently long.

Double Overhand/Double Figure-eight

After you have arranged a belay anchor, you must tie into it. Since you are already tied into the end of the rope, you must use a knot for the middle of the rope – a middleman's knot. (Mind you, this does not infer that you must tie in at the very middle of the rope. Rather, a middleman's knot simply refers to a knot tied into the rope anywhere but at the two ends.) For this purpose, two knots, the double overhand and the double figure-eight, provide the strength and ease of tying that make their use exclusive for the main tie-in to the anchor. The double overhand is the simplest knot imaginable, but once weighted can be a bearcat to untie. The double figure-eight, often just called a figure-eight, is better – strong and easy to untie.

Double Overhand (above), and Double Figure-Eight (below)

Clove Hitch

A tie-in knot that is quick and easy to tie, easy to adjust for length once tied, and unties easily is naturally a knot welcomed by climbers. The clove hitch is such a knot. It is particularly useful in constructing multi-nut anchors. The trade-off for all this utility is less strength than other knots. Clove hitches reportedly slip at around 1,000 pounds of load. This slipping can actually improve equalization of the load between the anchors, and help absorb energy from a leader fall, but may not be good for the rope. Clove hitches also have a tendency to work loose. Be sure they are kept tight at the bottom of the carabiner, away from the gate.

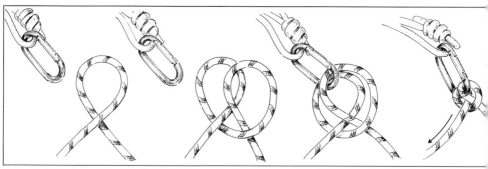

Clove Hitch; the arrow shows the load strand.

The reliability of a clove hitch can be improved by using a locking carabiner. I need to make an esoteric point here about clove hitches. The load strand of the rope coming from the clove hitch should be aligned near the spine of the carabiner, and away from the gate, or you sacrifice nearly one third of the carabiner's strength. The clove hitch should not be used as the sole tie-in knot – the wise climber uses a figure-eight somewhere in the anchor system. I have never heard of a properly tied clove hitch failing in any climbing situation; likewise, carabiner failure is almost unhead of as well. Still, you might as well be apprised of the considerations.

Knot now in hand, be certain never to tie off an anchor with only one carabiner. That simply is relying too much on a piece of equipment that can easily hide flaws – and the gate might get torqued open by a bight of rope. A slim chance, granted, but you don't want to take any chances, so you use two carabiners, gates opposed, or better yet, a locking carabiner and a regular back-up carabiner.

A Tri-cam (A) opposed against a SLCD (B) in vertical cracks. After the single clove hitch was tied into each of the carabiners, the SLCD was pushed down the crack until both pieces were tensioned against one another. The climber would clip into the end of the sling, or tie it off with an overhand knot and clip into the shorter loop to get closer to the anchors.

PRO. This setup keeps the nuts tight against one another, especially when loaded, improving the security of the Tri-cam.

CON. To make this bomber, you need a sling, and the pieces must be just the right distance away from each other.

Same pieces as shown on the photo opposite, but the SLCD is set further away from the Tri-cam, so two clove hitches are used in the sling to tension the pieces against each other. This has the same pros and cons as the neighboring setup.

Anchor Dynamics

CHAPTER 8

NUTS IN OPPOSITION

Placing oppositional nuts becomes necessary when rope drag or side pressure could potentially dislodge a one-directional nut, or when the placement is the multi-directional element of a belay anchor. As implied by the name, opposition involves setting two nuts to work against each other. Sounds complicated, and it often is.

On the lead, you will often run into this scenario: You're going up a thin flake, but presently, you must traverse off right. You set a nut at the top of the flake, but you see straightaway that the traverse will put an oblique stress – a sideways pull – on the nut, which is slotted for downward pull. In short, the sideways pull could jockey the nut right out, no matter how many runners or quickdraws you put on it. The normal solution is to place an up-slotted nut and attach it to the down-slotted, load-bearing nut.

Like this solution on the lead, oppositional principles are no less important for belay anchors. Even if the direction of pull will come from only one direction – say, upwards from the initial belay anchor on the deck – an oppositional ground anchor makes the belay superior. An oppositional anchor will keep steady tension on your principal nuts, keeping them securely lodged. Also, it will create a multi-directional setup, so the belayer can move about a little to fix a snag in the line, reach for a water bottle, or whatever, without worrying about dislodging the nuts. Any way you shake it, a multi-directional anchor is superior to a one-directional anchor every time, offering more flexibility and far more security. The trick is how you attach the "keeper" nut to the other nuts in the system.

Opposition can be rigged in a vertical, horizontal, or even diagonal crack.

Essentially, four situations can arise in establishing opposition:

1. You can't find adequate placements at the right distance and the nuts are so close together that they can't hold each other taut. In this case, the best you can do is clip both the nuts together with a carabiner. When possible, use two carabiners with gates opposed, because of the dangerous tri-axial loading on the carabiners caused by this arrangement. Each of the placements must be fairly stable, as no real tension will be placed on the nuts to hold them tightly in place.

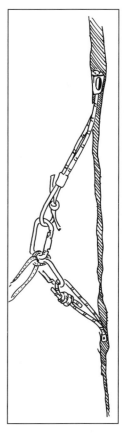

Nuts in opposition, tied together with a clove hitch on a sling.

2. The ideal situation: The nuts are at the right distance from each other, so they provide mutual tautness when cinched with two clove hitches on a ⁹⁄₁₆ inch or ⅝ inch sewn sling. After rigging this setup, clip into the sewn loop or one of the pieces, whatever best suits the overall anchor setup.

3. The nuts are very secure and don't need to be held taut, so the easiest solution is to simply clip both pieces into the same sling to create a multi-directional anchor. It might be best to arrange the sling to equalize the load with a sliding knot, which will be covered in the next section.

4. The available nut placements are too far apart, so the pieces must be held together with clove hitches in the climbing rope or a section of cordage. This works, but make sure you analyze the setup well, and crank those clove hitches tight so the nuts hold each other in place.

There are many other possible configurations for opposing nuts – far too many to run down here. The important thing is to understand the few rules of thumb we have laid down: Opposition, tautness, adjusting the length of slings, etc. Exactly how you rig any anchor is ultimately your call. Experience will teach you much, and always watch for innovative and slick setups other climbers may rig. You are never too old to learn a new trick.

Also, always double-check your partner's work, watching for poor or sloppy anchors, and don't be afraid to insist on better anchors if they don't look good. Many climbers set sloppy anchors, and it's up to the rest of us to set them straight before the Grim Reaper pays a visit.

Horizontal Oppositon

For a nut placed in a horizontal crack to be any good, it must be capable of withstanding some downward pull on the cable or sling, which will result in an outward pull on the nut. This means some part of the crack must taper at the lip, allowing you to wiggle a nut into place and hope it doesn't shift around and work loose from rope drag. It's often hard to clean these types of placements. When the crack does not taper at the lip, one option is to place oppositional nuts. This setup appears much more in climbing books and articles than it does in the field, however, because unless you have two ideal slots closely positioned, it is fairly tricky (and almost always very time-consuming) to rig horizontally opposed nuts that are any good. The advent of SLCDs has greatly reduced the need to consider horizontal oppositional nuts, but not eliminated the technique altogether.

The techniques described above for normal opposition generally work well for horizontal opposition, but in some situations, horizontally opposed nut setups are dicey and problematic. The difficulty is this: Somehow, you must rig two opposing nuts – both good for a lateral pull – so they also are good for downward loading. If you have two opposing

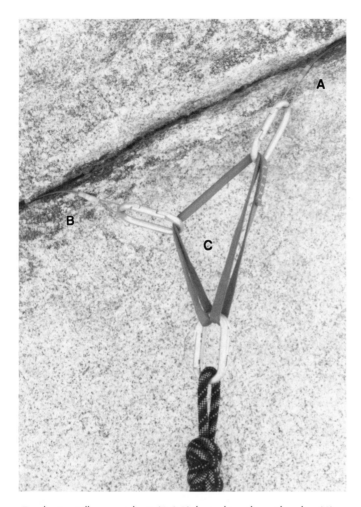

Two horizontally opposed nuts (A & B), looped together with a sling (C).

PRO. Understand this: There is no hard and fast law that we can lay down per just what to do here. Everything is relative to the situation, which differs greatly from anchor to anchor. To ensure security, the first thing you must do is eyeball the nuts and determine from which direction they can withstand the greatest pull. Here, the best guide is to consider the wires arrows pointing in the direction the given nuts will withstand the greatest impact. The next and all-important task is to rig the system so, in this instance, a downward pull will impact the nuts in the most ideal angle relative to their position (the direction the wires point). This setup is OK to the extent that it accomplishes this.

CON. As is, the upper nut (A) must sustain the bulk of any load. (B) is effective only because, by pulling slightly at (A), it redirects the loading onto (A) at the best angle. Still, I don't like the looks of this rig. Better opposition between the two nuts is needed. A good solution would be to rig the sliding knot on a short sling. Better yet, oppose the nuts against each other with two clove hitches in the sling. Remember, so long as you have an "uphill" nut — as in (A) here — that nut will absorb most of the force no matter how you rig the tie-off.

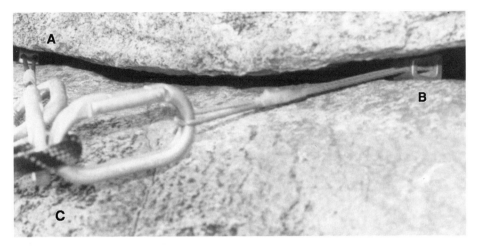

Two oppositional wires (A & B), clipped off short with biners (C).

PRO: Generally, you want to rig a system so the load is put on the nuts in the direction they can best sustain that load, and here is a rare example where the both nuts are absolutely bomber because they are set up to oppose each other.

CON: Extending the tie-in would decrease the angle of pull, and decrease the amount of opposition between the nuts. Also, you never want to clip nuts off short to each other like this because it puts an oblique stress on them both.

bottleneck placements, the nuts are probably good, and their placements easy, so it becomes a matter of rigging the tie-in so the nuts sustain a downward and inward pull.

Again, the ideal situation involves tying the two nuts taut against each other with clove hitches on a sling, and clipping into the sling. If the sling is fairly long – so the two legs of the sling from the nuts to the tie-in carabiner form a shallow angle – then the nuts must be able to withstand a force that pulls them both inward, toward each other and down, toward the load. If the pieces cannot withstand much of a downward force, using a shorter sling forces the loading more inward, but also increases the magnitude of the force because the pieces must work more against each other.

Some climbers simply connect the two nuts together with a chain of two or three carabiners. While this may be appropriate in some situations, it does put dangerous tri-axial loading on the tie-in carabiner, and forces the loading inward, which may be good for the stability of the pieces, but also may create unnecessarily high forces on them. Furthermore, the carabiner chain does not provide the oft-needed tautness to hold the pieces in the crack when they aren't loaded. If you must use a chain of carabiners, it's best to use two carabiners with gates opposed at the tie-in point.

Whatever the setup, horizontally-opposed nuts are only as good as the weakest nut. Ultimately, the only way to be sure is to test them with as violent a tug as is prudent, which, in fact, is a far cry from the forces exerted by a fall. However well we explain things here, placing horizontally opposed nuts takes a lot of practice. You're off to a good start, provided you understand and heed the basics.

EQUALIZING ANCHORS

Once you reach a belay stance, your first task is to put in one bombproof nut to tie in to. Once this bombproof anchor is in, you're secure enough to begin placing and equalizing other nuts, eventually creating an anchor that meets all the important specifications.

The principal reason for equalizing the anchors is to spread any potential impact force among the component parts of the anchor, reducing to almost zero the possibility that the whole works will fail. We've all had nuts rip out; some of us have had two nuts rip out. But I've never heard of an entire, well-equalized anchor failing altogether. Four or five bomber nuts, judiciously equalized, simply are not going to fail no matter how far a leader might fall on them, because that leader can generate only so much impact force, and a good, viable anchor can, and routinely does, sustain it.

By using oppositional elements in the anchor, and properly equalizing them to the principal, bombproof anchors, the anchor becomes multi-directional. You can yank and tug and fall on it from any angle and that baby will still hold. That's the bottom line with a belay anchor – it must hold, no matter what.

Robert Chisnall, in the Ontario Rock Climbing Association's *Rock Climbing Safety Manual* (1985), has made a complete study on the science of equalizing anchors, replete with graphs and equations that would vex Isaac Newton, plus various rope and knot configurations that I've never seen or even heard about in twenty-two years of cragging. However, the basic notions are invaluable.

The ideal equalized anchor should:

- Distribute the load evenly between the component parts of the anchor system;
- Have a minimum of slack between the various tie-in points;
- Be capable of self-adjusting, or automatically redistributing the load as the loading direction changes (say, as the belayer shifts position, or the belayed climber pitches off and swings);
- Be quick and easy to set up and dismantle;
- Employ generic gear on the leading rack (normal nuts, SLCDs, slings and biners).

Basically, there are two kinds of equalizing systems: static, pseudo-equalizing systems and automatic equalizing systems. The following pages, photos and commentary explain these principals in detail, but to start out, understand these short definitions:

- A static equalizing system refers to a grouping of nuts, pitons, bolts, etc. which are tied off together, with no slack in the system. For example, if we have four nuts in line, and tie them all off taut to each other, the impact force will, to some degree, get distributed over all four nuts.

This system does not provide perfect equalization, so some of the anchors are inevitably loaded more heavily than others.

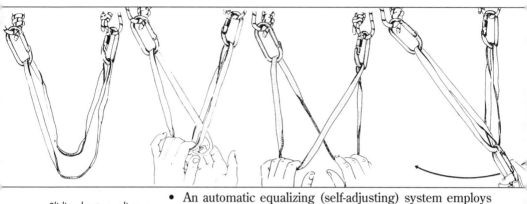

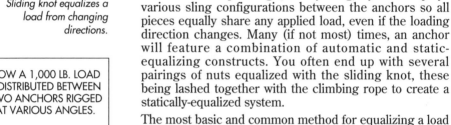

Sliding knot equalizes a load from changing directions.

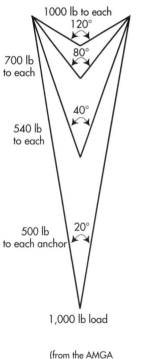

HOW A 1,000 LB. LOAD IS DISTRIBUTED BETWEEN TWO ANCHORS RIGGED AT VARIOUS ANGLES.

1000 lb to each
120°

700 lb to each
80°

540 lb to each
40°

500 lb to each anchor
20°

1,000 lb load

(from the AMGA Guides Manual 1992)

• An automatic equalizing (self-adjusting) system employs various sling configurations between the anchors so all pieces equally share any applied load, even if the loading direction changes. Many (if not most) times, an anchor will feature a combination of automatic and static-equalizing constructs. You often end up with several pairings of nuts equalized with the sliding knot, these being lashed together with the climbing rope to create a statically-equalized system.

The most basic and common method for equalizing a load between two pieces involves using a sliding knot on a sling. A proper twist in the equalizing sling is essential to prevent failure of the complete system if one piece pulls. Always double check to be sure that this twist is in place. This technique provides true automatic equalization; the drawback is that it can allow significant extension in the system if the slings are long and one of the anchors fails. To minimize the potential extension in longer equalizing slings, tie an overhand knot in the long leg of the sling, just above the tie-in point. Make sure the angle between the two legs of the sling is not too large, or the force on the anchors will be dramatically increased. An angle of about 25 degrees as shown in the sliding knot drawing works well. If the angle is larger than about 45 deprees, use a longer sling to decrease the angle.

Use of a cordelette greatly facilitates equalizing the load between two, three or four anchors. A cordelette is a 16-foot section of 6MM Spectra commonly used by guides to create a single point for connecting clients to all the individual anchors of a belay or toprope anchor system. This technique is especially useful for large parties, or when one climber is doing the majority of leading. The cordelette minimizes the number of carabiners, slings and quickdraws required to connect the anchors together (unless you just use the rope), thereby justifying its size and weight. To top things off, a cordelette is almost invaluable in self-rescue situations.

The cordelette is tied into a loop with a grapevine knot and clipped into each of the anchors. A loop of the perlon is

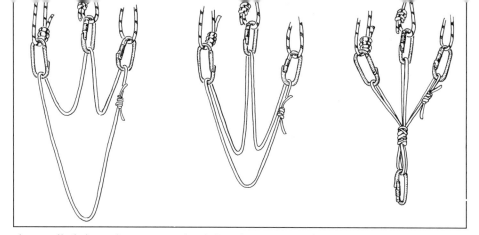

then pulled down between each of the pieces. If you have three pieces in your anchor, you'll get three loops that must then be pulled tight toward anticipated loading direction. Align the grapevine knot so it is near one of the pieces, away from the tie-in point. Next, tie an overhand knot, or if you have enough slack, a figure-eight knot, near the tie-in point and clip into the newly created triple loop. The cordelette has formed three separate, redundant loops that offer no extension if one of the anchors fails. The biggest shortcoming of this system is that it doesn't maintain perfect equalization if the loading direction changes. With practice, rigging anchors with cordelettes becomes quick and straight forward. While the cordelette is probably the best setup, and in time may well become standard, it is as yet still a novelty amongst most climbers who for the most part opt for a simpler, if less effective construct.

The cordelette equalizes multiple anchors with a single tie-in point.

A triple-length sling (13 to 14 feet) also works to equalize the load between three anchors, but you'll find perlon cord seems to work better.

Equalizing anchors is always advisable, but more elaborate methods are needed when the individual nuts are less than bomber. When all the nuts are good ones, and often they are, the simpler, static setup is usually adequate, and in actual practice, is normally used. Tying into each of the anchors with the rope, leaving no slack between them, is often the quickest and least gear-intensive way to set up a belay. Linking the anchors to a common point using slings of the appropriate length is a more gear-intensive and complicated setup. Often, a combination of these techniques is used to solve the problem at hand. Remember that these methods don't provide perfect equalization, especially if the loading direction changes, but they work well for connecting rock-solid anchors together.

There are a slew of involved and complicated equalizing configurations that have some value in big rescues, but are nearly worthless for recreational climbing purposes because of their impracticality. An automatic-equalizing system involves various sling and knot configurations nearly impossible to clearly depict in print without confusing everyone, including myself. For this reason, the many photos and attending commentary (found later in the book) remain our exemplary guide.

Belay anchors can be loaded in any direction. If the second climber falls, or if the leader falls before placing lead protection, the anchors will be loaded downward. Otherwise, the anchors will be loaded toward the first piece placed by the leader (provided the piece holds); thus the anchor system must be multi-directional.

When it isn't, bad things can happen. One instance immediately comes to mind.

My friends George Meyers and Kevin Worrall were climbing the Direct North Buttress on Middle Cathedral, a long, grade 4 free climb. More than a thousand feet up the wall, Kevin gained a small ledge – a mere stance, really – and set an anchor consisting of a web of wired nuts slotted in wee cracks on top of and behind the ledge. Since the whole works were good only for a downward pull, Kevin lashed off with runners and belayed in slings hanging below the ledge. George gained the belay, and took off for the next lead. With George some seventy five feet above, Kevin's legs cramped, and to relieve them, he stood up a little too high in his slings. The moment his waist (the tie-off point) came level with the ledge and the one-directional anchor, the direction of loading changed, the nuts popped en masse and Kevin found himself pitching down the wall, desperately trying to clasp the rope to break his fall. It's a wonder George wasn't pulled off when Kevin finally slammed onto the end of the rope, his hands so grooved and burned it took the whole summer for them to fully heal. Kevin became very adept at placing multi-directional anchors after that.

The most obvious multi-directional anchors are trees, chockstones and holes in the rock girth-hitched with a sling. Bolts and pitons also are multi-directional. Remember to be sure the tree is alive and well-rooted, the rock cavity or chockstone is solid, and the bolt is well-placed and in good shape – so far as you can tell.

As mentioned, oppositional placements also provide multi-directional capabilities. Horizontal cracks can sometimes work without opposition if they open in the back to accept a taper, but pinch at the edge to hold it against any direction of pull. A SLCD placed in a horizontal crack may also provide a somewhat multi-directional anchor. In a pinch, a SLCD set in the lower half of its expansion range in a vertical crack can be aligned with its stem pointing out to swivel toward the direction of pull. Though definitely not manufacturer-recommended, SLCDs usually can swivel ninety degrees or less without loosing their integrity if the crack is strictly parallel-sided, with no openings for the unit to walk into. A well-set Bigbro also can serve as a multi-directional anchor in a horizontal or vertical crack.

Provided you understand the basic concepts, and know how to rig the sliding knot and use the figure-eight and clove hitch, you should get by well, and safely.

Customizing Your Anchor

CHAPTER 9

TOPROPE ANCHORS

Toprope anchors must hold a load that is generally downward, but some sideways pull may also occur. Forces on a toprope anchor never approach those possible on a belay anchor, but can reach 800 pounds or more due to the addition of weight from the belayer and dynamic loading in the system. When setting toprope anchors:

- Evaluate any hazards at the site, especially loose rocks that the movement of a running rope could dislodge.

- Extend the anchors over the edge at the top of the cliff to prevent rope drag and damage. Two or more independent sets of slings should be used. Pad any sharp edges at the lip. Make sure the rope sits directly above the climb.

- If one or more of the anchors isn't near the edge of the cliff, a piece of climbing rope or a long sling can be invaluable for connecting anchors and extending them over the edge. Make sure to run two independent strands of rope or webbing over the lip to maintain redundancy.

- Set the chocks fairly close together near the top of the climb when possible to reduce the number of slings and carabiners required.

- Avoid setting pieces behind detached blocks, flakes or other questionable rock features. Also, avoid having the rope or the climber near these features.

- Connect the rope to the anchors with two opposed carabiners, at least one of which is locking. If a spare locking carabiner isn't available, be sure the gates are opposed, and add a third carabiner if you're paranoid! I have done my share of toproping, and whenever a locking carabiner is unavailable, I always triple the carabiners.

- Belay toprope climbs from the ground whenever possible. It's more fun and easier to watch the climber, and far easier to micro-feather the belay if you can anticipate falls. (And falls should be expected. That's the very reason you rig a toprope in the first place.) Avoid belaying directly below the climber, in case rocks come off. The force increases as you move away from the wall, so make sure you're anchored if you're not near the wall, or if the climber is built like Mike Tyson, and you're a slender little chap. The anchor merely needs to provide extra ballast to help you counterweight the climber, so two bombproof pieces are usually sufficient. If you're in an exposed situation, set up a redundant anchor system. An anchored belayer is a sitting duck for loose rocks, so don't be lashed into a shooting gallery.

Lastly, toprope anchors do pop on occasion. Several factors contribute. There's a nonchalant air about most all toproping, since, in theory, it's a totally harmless vocation. This nonchalance can spill over to the anchor set up, with climbers being satisfied with something less than bomber. People can be impatient to get climbing, and get lazy with the setup. The most common danger is to trust old slings on a long-standing toprope anchor – clipping into the slings, rather than rigging a safe setup off the anchors themselves. Not good. When a toprope anchor fails, it's a very ugly affair. Generally, there's a crowd at the bottom, eagerly awaiting their turn. All eyes are on the present climber. He pops, and splashes into the deck at your very feet. That can sour the sunniest day at the most enchanted crag. Take the extra time and rig it right.

BELAY ANCHORS

There are several techniques that accomplish the desired end of having a bombproof belay anchor, and a climber had best have a working understanding of them. Adaptability, versatility and innovation are keys to safe and convenient setups. Belay anchors can be subjected to loads upward of 2,000 pounds. Setting good belay anchors is unquestionably one of the most important safety steps in all of climbing, so never take shortcuts!

All experienced climbers go through a step-by-step process when rigging a belay anchor. The details of the procedure vary with the circumstances, but most everyone starts by looking for the most obvious anchor that can be arranged. Beginning and intermediate climbers sometimes will be enchanted by highly-decorative, exotic and obtuse anchors. Likewise, they may go out of their way (and waste time) to avoid the obvious, more secure and straightforward anchors so they can employ a trick setup, or an obscure piece of gear. This is not the way to go about it.

The first step is to locate where you want to belay – what physical location is best for tending the line, what affords the best stance, what allows use of the remaining gear on your rack, etc. If adequate anchor placements aren't available, consider moving the station higher if possible, or lower if necessary. Often, you won't have a choice. There will only be a small shelf, or one crack. In that case, you look for the best, most obvious big nut you can arrange. Most belay anchors are built around one atomic bombproof nut – a primary anchor. If there is more than one such placement, go with the one that is more handily located, ideally about chest level, where you can remain standing, can hang the rack, and can keep an eye on the whole works. Sometimes, you'll have

Pete Takeda and Jeff
Perrin on Aurora, El
Capitan.

photo: Greg Epperson

to rig the anchor at your feet, or off to one side, or wherever
the good placements are, then tie yourself off with slack
enough to get back in position to belay (always tying off taut
and in line with the direction of pull). Whatever the situation
is, the first priority is to sink that first, bombproof nut. If
you're at a dicey stance, you might want to clip into this piece
before you finish rigging the belay anchor.

The second step is to shore up the primary nut with
secondary anchors. Set one nut to oppose the primary nut
and create a multi-directional placement, then set at least two
more pieces in the downward direction to back up the
primary bomber. Remember that you want an efficient
anchor, not simply one that will bear the most impact. That

means the nuts should be straightforward to place and remove, and should be as centrally located as possible; a nice, tight grouping, as opposed to a baffling web of nuts crisscrossing the station. Once that first, primary nut is set, try to rig the secondary anchors in close proximity, but not so close that they are cramped or virtually on top of each other. If the rock is less than perfect in quality, you may want to spread the anchors out to preserve redundancy. Don't put all your eggs in one basket! Be sure the one closest to you (first to be loaded in event of an upward pull) is multi-directional.

Personally, I like to place a minimum of four pieces, three in the downward direction and one upward, opposing the primary anchor – no matter how inviolate the placements seem individually. Sometimes, three are enough, and sometimes that's all you'll get. Anything less is a crap shoot.

Lastly, you must connect the various components of the system together so they function as one unit. In many cases, this is the most critical, and difficult, part of the whole procedure. Several possibilities exist for connecting the anchors. In the best situation, the belayer will tie tightly to a bombproof multi-directional anchor set near his/her waist, then tie in to two more bombproof downward anchors placed above the first, with the belayer's body in line between the anchors and the anticipated direction of pull. Just remember ABC: Anchor, Belayer, Climber. It's a good idea to tie into the most bombproof anchor with a figure-eight knot, while clove hitches should suffice for the remaining anchors. It takes some practice to learn just how to feather the clove hitches so the whole rig is more or less under equal tension.

This popular rope tie-in is usually the quickest method, requires the least amount of extra gear, and is used ten to one over all other set-ups. Equalizing the anchors with a cordelette spreads the load most evenly, maximizing the overall strength of the anchor system, and reduces the belay switch-over time if one climber is leading all of the pitches, or if the party consists of more than two climbers. But again, the cordelette rig is a speciality setup that in actual practice few climbers can be bothered to rig (though it is probably the strongest one going).

If the anchors are spread out horizontally, try a hybrid system of connecting the system with slings and the rope. If you're low on slings and carabiners, tie the climbing rope into the anchors with a triangle system, running the rope through each of the anchors, then back to yourself so you are tight to all the anchors. This uses a fair amount of rope that may be needed if the next pitch is long, but the belayer could dismantle the last leg of the triangle to free a bit more rope at the end of a long pitch, if need be. If you have led the pitch with double ropes, connect one rope into the anchors on the right, and the other rope into the anchors on the left, to stay tight to all anchors.

If suitable anchors can't be found, it may be possible to climb to a higher placement to set up the belay, then climb back down to the belay ledge. Tying into the rope coming down from the high piece provides a backup to the available anchors. As a last resort (emergencies only!) it may be required of both climbers to climb simultaneously until the leader arrives at a suitable belay stance. This is potentially very dangerous – if the second falls, he/she will pull the leader off. "Simul" climb only on easy terrain, as a last resort. That's the law. If you get stuck on grim terrain and have to "Simul" to the only anchor, vaya con Dios.

If the belay anchors are less than bomber and no better possibilities exist – like on the double $\frac{1}{4}$ inch bolt belays still found on many slab routes – the leader should avoid clipping into the anchors before leaving the belay. If the leader clips the anchors and falls before setting another piece, the pulley effect increases the impact force on the belay anchors by almost two-thirds. No addition of force occurs if the leader is caught directly by the belayer, but the fall may be more severe for the leader, and is almost always a more grievous "catch" for the belayer.

Let's look at a theoretical situation, and go through the steps.

You lead a pitch up a hand crack that ends at a good stance. The crack continues above. You place a principal, bombproof nut and oppose it with another nut at waist to chest level, and tie yourself off taut, using a figure-eight. Other knots will do, but the figure-eight is the most proven, and the easiest to untie, once weighted. You place two more nuts above the first, and tie into each one with a clove hitch, adjusting the rope so each of the anchors is tight into the system. If properly rigged, each nut will share some of the load, and if one of the nuts pops, the absence of slack in the system keeps the impact from shock loading onto the other nuts. This, again, is our static, pseudo-equalizing belay rig. Furthermore, to ensure that any impact will indeed be spread about the various nuts, you face the anchor, and run the rope through one of the nuts above your belay device to belay, so it is easier to hold your struggling second.

That is far and away the most common setup.

RAPPEL ANCHORS

Perhaps the most gruesome of all climbing stories is the case of the climber, high on a big wall, rappeling back down to a hanging bivouac after fixing a pitch. He raps off the end of the rope, and windmills down into the void. Though this has happened, it is extremely rare. Far more frequent (though still very rare) is the case of the rappel anchor failing.

A climber named Nick Dibbler once had to rap off the second pitch of the Left Side of Reed's Pinnacle, in Yosemite, when his second couldn't follow the nasty offwidth. Rather than rig a decent anchor, and return later to clean it, Nick, infamous for his devil-may-care attitude, simply rapped off an old fixed bong (a large piton). He got about ten feet down the offwidth pitch and the bong popped. Screaming down the overhanging wall, the solo bong-bong flapping around above him, God Himself reached down and flipped the bong back into the crack, whence it miraculously lodged – end-wise – in the only constriction on the whole route. Nick wrenched to a halt, upside down, but alive. Nick's a priest in Guatamala now, I think.

Rappeling is probably the most dangerous procedure in all of climbing, even though no actual climbing is involved. For this reason, extreme caution should always be paid to any and every rappel, particularly toward the anchor.

Rappeling forces you to rely completely on your equipment and the anchors. Walking is usually the safest mode of descent, but rappeling may be necessary, or more convenient. Don't take any chances with your rappel anchors – they must also conform to the SRENE concept. Check the integrity of existing anchors. Sometimes rats or other varmints will chew on fixed webbing, so check the entire length of any existing slings in the system. Also, aluminum rappel rings can be worn through, especially in soft sandstone areas (sand gets in ropes and abrades the aluminum ring). Always inspect the rings, and back them up when possible. The rings can be backed up with a second ring, or just a loop of webbing that the rope passes through but doesn't load. Don't toprope off aluminum rappel rings, either – use a locking carabiner instead. Avoid the sloppy habit of trusting whatever fixed gear exists. Back up existing anchors if you have any question. Don't save a dollar and be a mother's lament!

At least two bombproof anchors should be established at rappel stations. Occasionally, rappel anchors consist of a single tree or set of slings on a rock feature, but climbers should back up anchors whenever possible. Anchors should be rigged using equalized slings, or at least slings of equal length.

A triangular sling configuration, sometimes called the American triangle, is commonly seen when two fixed anchors are side by side – two bolts on a smooth wall, two pitons driven into a horizontal crack, etc. A sling is fed through the two anchors, which form two points of the triangle. The third point of the triangle is where the rope or biner passes through the sling, at the bottom of the setup. There probably is not a cliff in America that doesn't sport this configuration, most likely as a popular, fixed rappel point. Considering that the physics are all wrong with this setup – it actually increases the load on each anchor – it's a wonder more of these rigs don't fail. As with other fixed anchors, you may well find an abundance of slings threaded through the anchor, climbers not realizing that it's not the slings that present the danger, rather the triangular rigging that so stresses the anchor.

Obviously, when the anchors are truly bombproof, it doesn't much matter how you tie them off. But anything shy of big new bolts should not be subjected to such inward loading as caused by a triangle: even the stoutest fixed pins will work loose after awhile, and to use the American triangle to connect passive anchors is to invite disaster.

The solution is easy. Tie the anchors off individually and rappel or belay from two or more slings; or equalize the force on them with the sliding knot.

Never run the rope around a chain or sling connecting the anchors. If one of the anchors fails, the rope simply pulls through and you're finished. Never lower from anchors with the rope running through a nylon sling, or the rope may burn through the sling and deposit you on the ground quicker than you can yell "Shiiiiiiit!" Rappeling with the rope running through slings is okay because the rope doesn't slide across the nylon slings when loaded, only when you pull to retrieve the ropes.

BIVOUAC ANCHORS

If you are bivouacked on a ledge, the main anchor is, of course, your main security, though you often will slot a couple of regional nuts if you're sleeping at a distance from the anchor, or at a place where you can't easily tie off taut to the main anchor (for instance, when the anchor is too far off to the side). Unless you're literally hanging over the edge, allow yourself enough slack so you can turn over in your bag, but not so much that you can roll off the ledge. Other considerations have to be worked out provisionally. It's mainly common sense.

Hanging bivouacs can get complicated, depending on the location, and the number of climbers and bags you have along. Since porta-ledges came into vogue about 15 years ago, the process has been greatly simplified. These are single-point suspension units, and most of the time, climbers simply tier them one above the other. If you're all on a steep, sheer wall, it's simple – you just clip off to the haul line that is tied to the anchor. But if you're in a dihedral, or if the rock is peppered with roofs or other features, you might have to spread out horizontally. In these situations, most climbers will climb off to the side and place a provisional anchor or a rivet to actually sleep from, with the main anchor providing the real security. Whatever you're sleeping from, make sure it's as bomber as the principal anchor. If your bivy anchor fails, you're in for a horrifying plunge, and at least an hour of grievous cocking around to get things right.

One of the most jackass fads to ever sweep Yosemite Valley passed through in the early seventies. I don't know what blockhead conceived it, but for a while, at the time when wall climbing was the rage, it was the vogue to see just how meager an anchor you could hang from for the night. You were backed up by an absolutely bombproof anchor, of course, but what you actually were hanging from was as dicey as you were foolish. Let me relate an few anecdotes to show how asinine this game was:

There was talk once that the great Canadian wall climber Hugh Burton had slept hanging from a Leeper hook. It was twenty years later that he told me he hadn't slept, so scared was he to even wink, lest the hook pop and his reputation be ruined. For my own part, I can remember being halfway up a new line in the Sierras, and slinging my hammock from a #1 Stopper. I was with Richard Harrison, who sleeps like Methuselah's father – deep and sound; but I've always slept like I was on deck for the gas chamber, more so when hanging from a harpstring and squashed into a hammock designed for people skinny enough to shower inside a flagpole. Who could ever really saw some quality logs in those blasted hammocks, anyhow? Not me. And when later that sleepless night Richard farted, or a carabiner shifted, or something caused some such noise, I can promise you Lazarus didn't vault out of his sarchopagus any faster than I got the hell out of that hammock and onto the main anchor. That fad was a short-lived one.

Lastly, no matter the particular anchor construct – bivouac, belay, toprope, rappel – the bottom line is that unless you make a habit of climbing on junk rock, or have a penchant for trashy routes, the vast majority of your anchors will be straightforward and easy to rig and clean. In actual practice, for instance, it is rare that an experienced leader will yell down "Off belay," and not yell "On belay" within a few short minutes, the belay anchor rigged and inviolate. There is no need to use the more involved and time-consuming anchor constructs when a simple rig will do. As mentioned, the elaborate oppositional and multi-equalized setups are normally called on only when the individual anchors (nuts, pitons, bolts, et al) are less than sound. Otherwise, always go with the easier setup. These are quicker, more practical, and much easier to assess and manage. Keep it simple. Nine times out of ten, simplicity equals safety.

In closing, let me reiterate that the anchor is the single most important part of the technical system. It is your first and last line of defense. Remember the Golden Rule: The anchor must be able to sustain the greatest load conceivable in a given instance, or it is not good enough. Heed this simple rule, climb high, and live long.

Anchor Analysis

After going through this chapter, every reader should understand that any anchor can be improved, shorn up, or made stronger, and that the notion of a "perfect" anchor is a theoretical abstraction for textbooks other than this one. Nothing is ever perfect in climbing but blue sky, warm rock and friends new and old. The science of understanding anchors is in knowing the handful of fundamental systems and routines we've laid down and illustrated in this manual; the art of sound anchors is in creating them on the cliffside. If you take nothing else away from this reading, take this: Unless an anchor can withstand the greatest impact force that can possibly be put to it in a given situation, the anchor is not good enough. The quickest, simplest, most straightforward method of achieving this end is always the anchor of choice. Good climbing!

Let's look at a variety of belay set ups, and learn as we go:

The next four photos show different possibilities for rigging a belay anchor from the same four nut placements.

(ABOVE): The minimalist approach simply uses the rope to tie into the anchors. A SLCD and bomber Hexentric (A) tied off tight with clove hitches to an oppositional nut below (B) and a backup SLCD above (C). The SLCD (A) is set so it shares the load with the Hexentric, and the gates of the two carabiners are opposed and clipped into both of the anchors. The belayer is tied into the strand of the rope coming down from (B). Note that the load strands of the clove hitches are oriented along the back spine of the carabiner, and the clove hitches are cinched nice and tight, with no strands on the gate of the biner. You might consider belaying the second through a biner connected into the two carabiners at (A), especially if you're expecting someone to struggle and hang on the rope.

PRO. This setup is quick and clean, and requires few carabiners and no slings.

CON. The block that the Hexentric and SLCD are placed behind is hollow sounding and has hairline cracks all the way around it; better to explore the solid rock a bit higher. The anchors are not perfectly equalized. The belayer may need another oppositional nut lower, or should tie in tighter to (B), to avoid being catapulted into the roof above if the leader takes a screamer.

(ABOVE): The team is using double 9MM ropes, so the belayer is tied into the anchors using both ropes. This improves the equalization in the system.

PRO. Like the setup on the opposite page, this is quick, clean and requires a minimal amount of connecting gear.

CON. The block is loose, and the system relies entirely on clove hitches. The belayer should be a little closer to (B).

(**ABOVE**): The two anchors at (A) are equalized with the SLCD at (C) using a sliding knot. The lower oppositional knot is still tensioned with a clove hitch in the climbing rope. The belayer could be tied into either strand of the rope, depending on the situation. The chocks at (A) share half of any downward load, while the SLCD at (C) must hold half of the load by itself. Belay the second through the carabiners that create the sliding knot.

PRO. Any load will be well-equalized among the anchors, increasing their overall strength, even if the loading direction changes slightly. The belayer is tied into the upper anchors with two opposed carabiners, one of which is locking. The equalizing sling actually consists of two slings for redundancy, and an overhand knot has been tied into the slings to minimize the extension if the anchors at (A) fail – which is likely to happen since the block is loose.

CON. This is a bit time-consuming to set up, and requires six carabiners and two or three slings. Again, the belayer needs to be tied in tight to the upward anchor.

(ABOVE): A cordelette has been used to equalize the load on each of the three downward anchors, and two clove hitches on the sling are used to tension the oppositional nut against the lowest of the three downward nuts.

PRO. This setup gives the best equalization, and therefore maximizes the overall strength of the system, provided the loading direction doesn't change very much. The cordelette also provides a single point for the team to connect into. An overhand knot has been tied in the three strands of the cordelette to minimize the extension if one of the anchors fails. Belay the second through the carabiner attached into the cordelette (D), or directly off the anchors at that point.

CON. This is time-consuming to rig, and requires use of a specialized piece of gear – the cordelette. The belayer is tied in with a single locking carabiner, which is OK in some circumstances, but two biners are always better.

 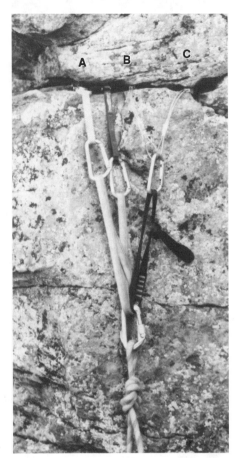

The three photos on these two pages show options for connecting the same pieces together into a belay anchor.

(LEFT): A SLCD (A) and a Tri-cam (B) are equalized with the sliding knot and backed up by two opposed tapers connected with a clove hitch on the climbing rope.

PRO. This setup is fairly quick and doesn't require much gear. Any load will be shared among the four pieces. A variety of gear was used to create this anchor. Because of the horizontal aspect of the crack, this setup could also hold an upward pull.

CON. The belayer will be lifted quite a bit before the leader impacts the anchors should he/she take a whistler, so an oppositional nut below is a good idea. On the other hand, if the belayer does get yanked up, it will decrease the impact on the top (lead) anchor. If the opposed tapers were much further apart, you might consider using two carabiners; this would reduce because of the triaxial loading on the carabiner.

(CENTER): Pieces (A) and (B) are still equalized, and the oppositional tapers (C) are extended to match the length of the sliding knot.

PRO. Shares the load nicely between three pieces, and the belayer is tied into the single-point anchor with two opposed carabiners, one a locker.

CON. Takes a few carabiners, two slings and a bit of extra time to rig.

(**ABOVE**): Anchors (A), (B) and (C) are equalized with a cordelette to create a single point anchor.

PRO. This system maximizes the overall strength of the anchors by spreading the load most evenly in the event of a downward load. With practice, this system becomes quick to set up.

CON. If the loading direction changes dramatically, the equalization in compromised. Requires a cordelette.

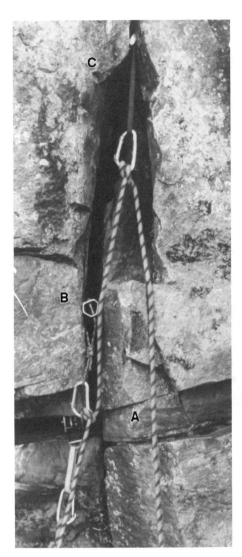
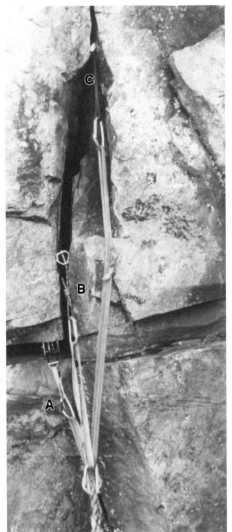

The photos on these two pages show options for connecting
together these three anchors.

(LEFT): The minimalist approach again, with the climbing rope
connecting the belayer to all three anchors. The SLCD (A) set in
the horizontal crack is tied into the rope with a figure-eight knot,
and is backed up by a bombproof Hexentric (B) and a Tri-cam
(C), both of which are tied off with easily adjustable clove
hitches.

PRO. This quick setup requires a minimum of gear – only three
carabiners – and a short section of the rope, and uses a variety of
chock types. The lowest anchor will hold any possible direction
of pull, and the rope is adjusted so the chocks share the load
fairly well. The belayer is tied into (A) with a figure-eight knot.

CON. The load is not perfectly equalized.

(CENTER): The SLCD (A) and the Hexentric (B) are equalized with a sliding knot, and the Tri-cam (C) is extended with a sling to a length where it is statically equalized with the other two pieces.

PRO. Quick to set up and creates a single-point anchor.

CON. Takes more time and gear than the setup in the first photo.

(ABOVE): The same three anchors are equalized with a cordelette.

PRO. This is a bombproof rig that maximizes the overall strength of the anchors, allowing the belayer to stay tied tight to the first anchor.

CON. Requires a cordelette; takes a little longer to rig and break down than the rope tie-in.

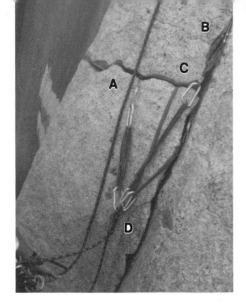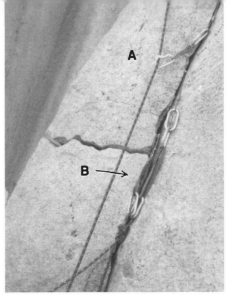

These photos show a variety of groupings of nuts behind the same leaning pillar.

(LEFT): The anchor consists of two nuts (A&B), and a sling over a flake (C) held in place by a "keeper" stopper. All three components are connected with slings so the tie-in point (D) is relatively balanced, distributing the load onto all three anchors.

PRO. A nice, tight grouping, easy to install and clean. The slings are arranged at a common length, so the load will be absorbed, to some extent, by all three anchors. The belayer is tied off with little slack, and all the anchors appear to be sound ones provided this leaning pillar is sound. If the top pillar toppled, the remaining anchor would be dust.

CON: I wouldn't be smiling until the leader got some bomber anchors in higher up, in a real crack, and not just behind this leaning pillar. Even then, the absence of an oppositional anchor beneath (A), (B) & (C) means the anchor is worthless for an upward pull, which is exactly where the force will come from once the leader sinks that first good piece. If the leader takes a long fall, especially early in the pitch, the belayer could be wrenched off her stance, resulting in an upward pull on the anchors. This problem is compounded if the leader substantially outweighs the belayer. The nut on the far left might hold some upward pull, but a piece lower in the crack to oppose the upper ones would ensure no chance of stripping all the belay anchors. The sling/keeper stopper arrangement also could be improved by equalizing the stopper into the tie-in point, so the nut takes half of any impact load. Applying pressure to the nut by tying it in also keeps the sling in place. Also, the lead rope doesn't run through the anchor. If the leader had slipped just off the belay, the entire load would land right on the belayer's Sticht plate. Not good. Note: Having the load of a leader fall come onto the anchors rather than the belayer creates a pulley effect that increases the impact load (on the anchors) up to 60%.

(CENTER): Various wired nuts (A), and a single tie-in point (B).

PRO: The nuts are somewhat equalized by the length of the slings. A quick setup.

CON: This is a dangerous setup because several wired nuts do not a sound anchor make. The belayer should be weeping bitterly, not laughing. No matter how good the wired nuts are, you simply need something more substantial for a bomber belay. A few SLCDs in the horizontal crack to the left would be a start. And, of course, you'd want to place a few oppositional nuts below, because otherwise, the only upward anchor is the belayer's 135 pounds (since the wires are no good for an upward pull). Once again, the detached pillar that the anchors are placed behind may not be sufficient to withstand a lead fall. In short, this anchor meets none of our requirements.

(ABOVE): An SLCD (A) and a sling (B), tied off with clove hitches (C).

PRO: There is nothing remotely acceptable about this anchor.

CON: The SLCD has a solid stem, and when placed in a horizontal crack, the stress can bend or even break it. Use a SLCD with a flexible shaft here. The sling (B) is probably more secure than a cobweb, but not much. Until the leader sinks that first bomber piece, any impact force will lift the belayer up, and there goes the sling. Two components are simply not enough for a good anchor, even if they were good ones, which they aren't. The belayer is not running the rope through the anchor, though I don't know as I blame her, because the last thing you'd ever want to do is to fall on such a pitiful mooring. Again, to compound matter, the pillar appears detached.

(ABOVE): Two SLCDs (A&C) and a wired nut (B) in a horizontal crack. Note that the two SLCDs are equalized with a single sling, forming an automatic equalizing system, and that an overhand knot has been tied to shorten the sling connecting the taper, which statically equalizes this piece with the SLCDs. Within reason, the longer the slings, the less the oblique loading on the SLCDs. There are more elaborate ways to equalize these nuts, but since each is truly bomber, and the system is rigged to spread most of the load over all three pieces, it's sound.

PRO: The crack is a good one, and the nuts are most likely bomber. The grouping is close and handy and the setup clean. Note that the gates of the biners are turned away from the rock, so any incidental contact cannot open them.

CON: The biggest problem here is that both SLCDs have their rigid stems over an edge. Flexible-stemmed devices would be far better here. Also, I always like at least four pieces for an anchor, but this is moot, since you can always improve an anchor. The genuine question is whether the system is good enough for the task at hand; and it would be here if the SLCDs had flexible stems. The belayer also could be tied in a little shorter, and could belay through the anchor so the nuts, not her brisket, will take any impact force. Also, the tie-in carabiners aren't opposed, and both carabiners should be clipped into both slings. This setup is good principally for a downward pull. If the leader is to carry on above, the anchor would have to be equalized, and you'd probably want to rig an oppositional anchor in the crack to the left and pull the whole works taut, just to keep everything from shifting. Her shades look a little over-sized, but she's otherwise in control.

(**ABOVE**): Two SLCDs (A), two wires, opposed and clipped off at a mutual point (B), and an SLCD (C) to belay through.

PRO: All of the individual placements are sound. The system is clean and compact, and slotting a SLCD to belay through is a good notion, because the belayer's stance is slightly to the right of the main anchor.

CON: There are several problems with the manner in which the components of this anchor have been connected. First, the two SLCDs (A) have been clipped off together, but there is at least a half-inch difference between the ends of the slings, so only the one with the shorter sling will absorb any loading. Second, there is too much slack between (A) and (B), reducing (A) to a mere back-up system; it would not take any of the load unless (B) were to rip out altogether. The two nuts at (A) need to be equalized, and (A) and (B) need to be equalized as well. The latter can most easily be accomplished by using a clove hitch at (B), and tying off taut to (A). Any time you must rig an anchor in an elliptical or arching crack, the challenge is to rig the system so the load is spread, if not evenly, at least partially over the various components. The load would be distributed most evenly using slings or a cordelette to equalize the load on each of the pairings of nuts. Finally, while it is a good idea to belay through a nut, one funk SLCD stuck in the underside of a flare is something less than bombproof. Shore it up with another, or rig the anchors better and belay directly off them.

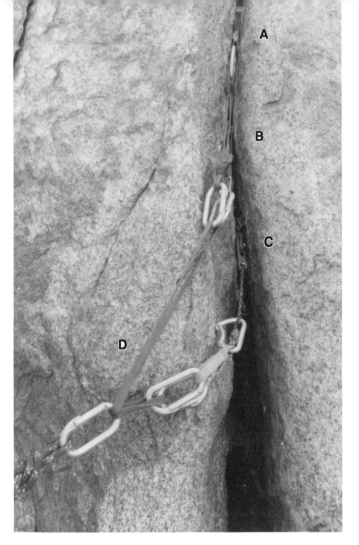

(ABOVE): Two wired nuts (A & B), and an SLCD (C), equalized with the sliding knot (D).

PRO: All the nuts are sound, judiciously clipped off and equalized.

CON: This is a perfect place for the sliding knot. The problem is that the quickdraw on (C) is just a little too long. When the anchor is weighted (in this example, it is not), the biners on (C) will creep flush to the tie-in biner and (C) won't share as much of the load as it would if it were clipped off a few inches shorter. Remember, whenever you use the sliding knot, or any self-adjusting equalizing setup, test the whole system by weighting it slightly and letting the rig settle in. Once that's done, you might want to make a few small adjustments to get things just right. This system does not include redundancy in the equalizing sling, and connecting to the whole anchor system with a single non-locking carabiner is ludicrous. Also, the gate of the carabiner connected to the higher of the two Friends is pressed against the rock.

(RIGHT): Two wired nuts (A), an oppositional wired nut below (B) connected to an upper nut via a sling/pulley rig (C). The top nut is connected with a sling (D), and the whole matrix is clipped off at a mutual point (E).

PRO. The upper two nuts are bombproof, and the lower directional nut (B) provides the anchor with multi-directional capabilities. The whole setup is compact, clean, and simple.

CON. Anytime you use a sling/pulley setup (C), you unnecessarily multiply the stress. If the second nut should fail, the oppositional nut will pull straight through, and you'll be left hanging from only the top nut. Your body will serve as a counterweight against a leader fall – when the leader has moved past this anchor and is above you. While on those rare, very long falls, forces might jerk the belayer up a bit, you rarely see a belayer yanked off a ledge like he/she was shot out of a cannon, because the stretch in the cord and the rope drag through gear inhibits these kinds of forces. For the most part, oppositional anchors are set both to keep the belayer from getting lifted up (in the event of great upward loading), and to keep the non-directional nuts lifted out. Normally, it is better to simply tie the directional anchor (B) off taut to the upper nuts. This accomplishes what's needed, and avoids the sling/pulley rig. Another problem: the gates on the biners are not opposed. I would add one more downward nut, and rig the upward directional nut tightly against the lowest downward nut using two clove hitches in a sling.

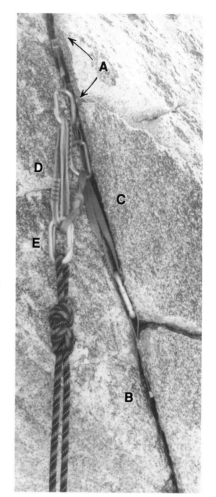

(LEFT): A cordelette is used to equalize the load on two tapers and an SLCD, and to provide opposition between the SLCD and the upward-directional Tri-cam.

PRO. This setup gets the maximum strength out of the smaller nuts. A belayer tied tight to these anchors isn't going anywhere. The single-point anchor is uncomplicated for large parties to clip in and out of, or if one climber leads most of the pitches.

CON. Takes more time to rig and requires a cordelette.

(RIGHT): The belayer is tied tight to the Bigbro with a figure-eight knot, and to the two upper SLCDs with clove hitches.

PRO. Quick to rig and requires a minimum of gear. The Bigbro is well set and capable of holding an upward pull from a falling leader.

CON. Requires the use of a lot of big gear, which may leave the leader short on the next pitch; but it appears there is no other choice.

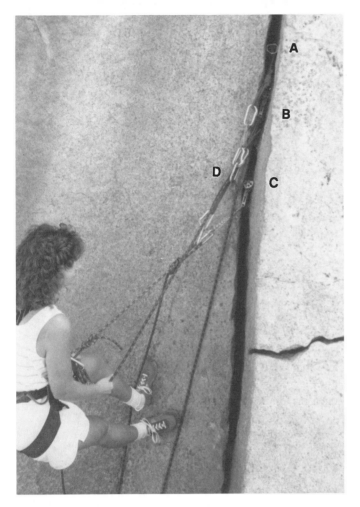

(ABOVE): A hanging belay consisting of a hex (A), two SLCDs (B), and another SLCD (C). The sling arrangement is a good example of a static-equalizing system. The rope is running through the anchor (D).

PRO: A satisfactory grouping of solid anchors, adequately tied off to distribute the load over the various nuts. Running the rope through the anchor makes it easier to hold the partner if he falls or hangs on the rope. The system is clean and strong.

CON: There is no oppositional nut, so when the leader continues above, the anchor is not adequate for an upward pull. One, or preferably two nuts below, tied off taut to the existing anchor, is the ready solution. Also, on any hanging belay, most climbers find it more convenient and even safer to be tied in a little closer to the anchor, so they can easily reach all the various components if they need to juke something around or free a snag. This anchor is bomber, but only for a downward pull. This setup also requires an excessive amount of gear – seven carabiners, a quickdraw and a sling – and quite a bit of time to set up. Tying in with the rope would only require three carabiners, and using a cordelette would require three carabiners and one locking carabiner.

(ABOVE): An SLCD (A) and two passive nuts (B) tied off at a single point (C).

PRO: The nuts are solid ones, and the system is rigged so all three pieces bear some of the load. Clean and simple.

CON: This anchor is not as good as it could be because of the absence of an oppositional anchor below, and because it is not perfectly equalized. The nuts in the horizontal crack (B) will absorb upward pull, but to make this anchor truly bombproof, you'd need to place a nut below the whole system and clip it off taut to the upper nuts or the belayer. We can't tell from this photo, but hopefully the leader placed a frank nut very soon after fleeing this belay.

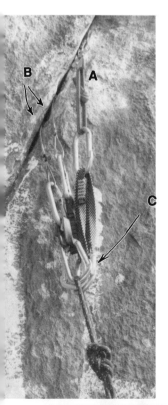

(LEFT): An SLCD (A), two wired nuts (B), clipped off at a mutual tie-in (C).

PRO: The nuts are as solid as thin nuts get. The setup is compact, neat and straightforward.

CON: The tie-in consists of three biners at the knot. While the slings converge at pretty much the same point, a difference of a quarter-inch in the length of the slings can mean that just one of those meager wired nuts might have to sustain the whole load. Not good. The smaller the nuts, the more crucial it is to equalize. At the very least, the wires should be equalized with the sliding knot, at best, with a cordelette. Clipping into a knot with any more than two biners is problematic, because when weighted the biners shift, and one or another is left to sustain the load. The whole anchor needs to be re-thought – backed up and equalized. This setup also provides no resistance to an upward pull after the leader climbs above the belay. Best to clean this whole mess and start over.

(**ABOVE**): A small SLCD (A) and a wired micro nut (B) constitute this "anchor."

PRO: Nothing at all.

CON: The idea that two wee nuts in a seam constitutes a viable anchor is an idea that will get you killed – quickly. Even if the belayer had equalized the nuts, they are still not nearly enough. And since there is no oppositional nut, this anchor is worthless for an upward pull, which is the only direction the pull will come from once the leader puts in some gear. If the leader were to fall here – which he looks close to doing – the impact would rip the anchor right out (provided the belayer's hip belay could hold such a fall, which is questionable), and the two dupes would shortly find themselves in the Golden City, harps in hand, wondering what went wrong.

(**OPPOSITE PAGE**): This features a grouping of four nuts – two SLCDs and two wired nuts. By the judicious use of biners and quickdraws, the system has been statically equalized: The slings and wires from all four pieces have been extended to meet at exactly the same spot – the tie-in point. (B) is an oppositional nut.

PRO: This is about as slick, compact and bomber a setup as you are likely to get in what is a pretty sketchy situation – a sling belay from small nuts. Without (B) (the oppositional nut), a fall would load the system from the side and the (A) matrix would be vulnerable to ripping out, no matter how good the nuts are. The distance at which (B) has been rigged to (A) keeps loading at a better angle. If you look closely and visualize where the impact force will come from – directly from the left side – you realize that a great deal of the load will be absorbed by the one oppositional nut (B).

CON: This is a situation where the belay anchors must be set to hold against two foreseeable directions of pull. When the belayer is leaning on the anchors, as he is here, while his partner is seconding the pitch below, the anchors must be able to hold a downward pull. As soon as that first piece is clipped by the new leader ascending left, the anchors must be shored up against a hard leftward pull in case of a fall. Because (B) (the oppositional nut) will absorb so much of the impact force in the event of a leader fall, it would be better to see one or even two more oppositional nuts rigged near (B). It also wouldn't hurt to have one more downward anchor. Always remember that a sling belay from wires and small SLCDs is a nervous affair; the only way to compensate for the reduced strength of the components is redundancy. On a popular route, a bolt would most likely be placed to shore up such an anchor, but not always.

This rigging distributes the load among the anchors, but not equally. If the downward-slotted chocks are less than bombproof, their overall strength will be maximized if everything is well-equalized. Also, by clipping the lead line into the belay anchors, the leader has set up a pulley effect that increases the force on those anchors, especially if he falls before placing the piece at the lip. After the piece at the lip is clipped, this setup places a large sideways impact on the leftmost nut, should the leader fall; this could pop the piece out, depending on the placement.

One final point: The gate of the carabiner connected to the middle nut faces the rock. Best turn it around so the gate cannot be pushed open, which sacrifices more than half of the carabiner's strength.

(ABOVE): A hanging belay consisting of two hexes (A & B), and an SLCD (C) tied off at one point (D).

PRO: Taken individually, the nuts are good ones.

CON: This is one of those places where a leader must be resourceful to get a bomber anchor. It is quite possible, however, because the nuts are good. The problem boils down to how the system is rigged, and this setup is precisely wrong. First, because the nuts are tied off so short – particularly the right one – a stout impact force will load the nuts at oblique angles, and they could fail. Hexes, unless slotted in a true bottleneck, usually are sound for a very limited range of angle. For example, the right nut in this setup is probably sound, provided the direction of pull is straight down. But pull at it from the side, and it's less than adequate. This system first needs to be equalized, and the slings extended, so the tie-in point is lower, thus decreasing the angle of oblique stress (inward pull) on the component nuts. A perfect place for the cordelette, which would extend the pieces and equalize the load. And again, there is no oppositional nut, so no matter how you rigged this anchor, it's only good for a downward pull. Personally, I find three nuts one short of a good hanging belay. I'd load up that lefthand crack with SLCDs, have several oppositional nuts below as well, then kick back and enjoy the view.

(ABOVE): Two SLCDs (A), two wired nuts (B) clipped off at one point, a clove hitch (C) tied between the two components, and the belayer is tied off to (C) with a clove hitch (D).

PRO: This is an almost perfect setup, making good use of the clove hitch. The two wires (B) are rigged so the pull is in line with the manner in which the nuts are slotted. By creating a loop between (A) and (B), and tying off with the clove hitch at (C), the load is equally distributed between (A) and (B). Since there is little slack in the system, the impact force will not shock load onto the other grouping of nuts in the event either (A) or (B) fails. (This does, however, leave the belayer to belay from a single clove hitch. Not good; it would be better equalized with a cordelette or slings.)

CON: The main problem with this setup is that at (A), one of the slings is longer than the other, so while they are clipped off at a mutual point, only the shorter-slung SLCD will absorb any force. A simple solution is to simply twist the sling on the righthand (longer) nut until it is the same length as the shorter sling to its left. Also, while this system is multi-directional, it is more effective for the downward, as opposed to upward, pull. Since there simply is no place to rig an oppositional nut below, the belayer could get lifted up by a severe upward pull. No doubt the anchor could sustain such a load, but ideally, you'd want an oppositional nut below so the anchor would remain dead static in the event of upward loading. Again, a leader must make do with what the rock affords, trying to make the anchor as bomber as possible. Rarely is the situation such that you can rig a textbook anchor, but this does not mean a safe one cannot be achieved.

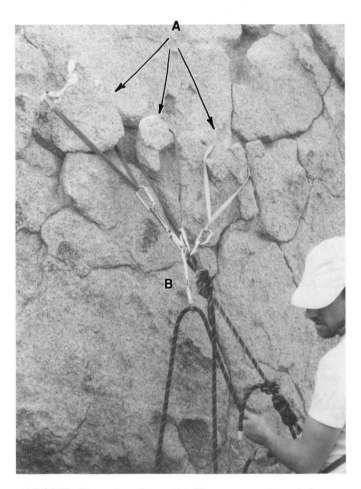

(ABOVE): Three slung horns (A). The rope runs through the anchor (B) for the belay.

PRO: The slings are long enough, and the horns spread out enough, that though not truly multi-directional, the system will withstand some loading from oblique angles – provided the slings don't pop. Note how each sling has been extended with quickdraws or biners and clipped in to a single point; the one-point tie-in creates a static-equalizing system.

CON: A more elaborate equalizing system might make the belay a little stronger and more multi-directional, but the main problem is that the horns themselves are poor for the job. If at all possible, you always want to tie-off a horn, rather than simply drape a sling over the top; otherwise, constant downward pressure is all that keeps the sling in place. As is, I'm not sure that one or more of the slings wouldn't rip right off those horns if suddenly impacted. Optimistically, this setup is a fair solution to a very dangerous situation. Only the center horn looks useable to me, and just barely. Nice to see the rope running through the anchor, but I question whether it would hold. And of course, if this setup is in fact any good at all, it is good only for a downward pull.

(**ABOVE**): Two slings over horns (A), extended with runners
(B), and clipped off at a mutual point (C).

PRO. Not much.

CON. Ask yourself just what forces this setup is designed to
withstand. Since the leader is above, the force will come directly
up the line of the rope – provided that the leader has placed solid
lead protection. Since the slung knobs are good only for a
downward pull, they are worthless. Remember, unless the
belayer is standing between the anchor and the cliff, a ground
anchor has to be multi-directional to be any good at all.

(ABOVE): Two SLCDs (A) and a horn (B).

PRO: Both the SLCDs and the horn are good. Note that the horn is not draped, but is tied off. The components of the anchor are bomber, and will probably never fail. The setup is clean and simple.

CON: Again, the rigging is inadequate. The horn should be tied off slightly taut to the SLCDs, and there should be no slack between the horn and the belayer. That done, any impact would get distributed more evenly between both the horn and the SLCD. As is, a fall would probably rip the belayer off his stance, and the horn would have to withstand the whole load. No doubt it could (if it isn't cracked all the way through), but by simply making a few simple adjustments on the rigging, this anchor could quickly become as secure as Fort Knox.

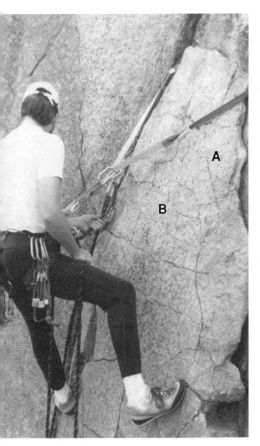 

(ABOVE LEFT): A sling over a flake (A), and an oppositional SLCD (B) to keep the sling in check.

PRO: The concept of using an oppositional nut (B) to hold the sling in place is a good and standard one, but there's little more to recommend this anchor.

CON: The main problem is (A), which looks about as secure as a lariat around a beach ball. Furthermore, the top of the flake looks like it's cracked through. Even if the flake was strong as the Rock of Ages, I'd go with two slings, just in case there were any sharp edges. This belay is rickety at best, though it's adequately rigged.

(ABOVE RIGHT): The same setup as above left, save the leader is now above the anchor.

PRO: Zero.

CON: Since any impact force will come from above, said force would be absorbed only by the belayer's weight and the one oppositional nut (B). Even if the sling was good – which it isn't – you'd want at least one more oppositional nut around (B) to take that upward load. The obvious solution is to drop down a body length and rig the anchor in the crack by the belayer's left boot.

(ABOVE LEFT): A tree tied off with the rope.

PRO: The tree is stout enough to withstand any possible force, and anchoring off to it is easier and safer than rigging any other anchor.

CON: The tree has sap and rough bark on it, neither of which is good for the rope. Also, remember to avoid relying on a single anchor unless it is bombproof beyond doubt, and you are willing to bet your life on it, which you are.

(ABOVE RIGHT): Same setup as above left, save that the belayer has tied off the tree with a sling.

PRO: As mentioned earlier, always sling a tree or any natural anchor with webbing, rather than the rope, for the simple reason that the sling is more than strong enough and is about 100 times cheaper than the cord.

CON: I always like to clip an anchor off not with one but two biners, gates opposed. And the belayer has got to lose that silly beard.

(ABOVE): A hanging belay from two bolts, which are clipped off with two slings and tied off at a mutual point.

PRO: This is the safest way to tie off to a bolt anchor because it avoids the belay triangle, in which the tie-in is closer to the bolts, and puts inward stress on them. The belayer is running the belay rope through the lefthand bolt, so it, rather than his waist, will absorb the load.

CON: The belayer has tied off long so he can be closer to the lip and can eyeball the climber seconding the pitch. The problem with tying off long – here, and at all hanging belays – is that the anchors are out of reach. Once the second gains the stance, he is left to tie himself off because the belayer cannot reach the anchors. It's always a trade-off with sling belays. The main concern is (usually) to rig the simplest and cleanest system that spreads the load out onto the component parts of the anchor. This belay also would be better if both tie-in carabiners, gates opposed, were clipped into both slings. If these bolts are anything less than absolutely solid, they should be equalized with a sliding knot, and the rope should run through the equalized point on the sliding knot before it runds down to the climber, rather than just to the lefthand bolt; if they are three-eighths of an inch in diameter and/or larger, and well-placed, this setup is adequate.

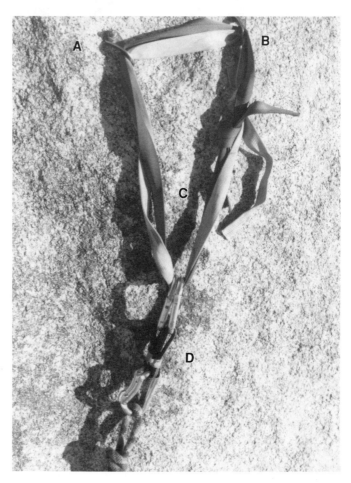

(**ABOVE**): Two bolts (A & B) connected by two runners in the American Triangle configuration (C), clipped off with two quickdraws (D).

PRO. The bolts are three-eighths inch. Bomber.

CON. Why clip off to a couple of tattered slings when you can clip straight into the bolt hangers? Research says that two slings, even really shabby ones, are unlikely to fail, but I've seen enough slings break to doubt this science. The solution is very easy: Tie off straight to the hangers. The only reason these slings were left behind is because somebody had to rappel off. This means at least one rope was doubled through the slings, and eventually pulled all the way through, which can generate friction enough to burn straight through the slings, or at the very least, significantly weaken them. Whatever, this is a skull-and-crossbones setup to be sure. Just clip off to the hangers. In addition, even if the slings are good, the quickdraws should be set up with carabiner gates opposed. Three-eighths-inch bolts (pictured) are not likely to fail, but if the bolts are anything less, you should avoid the "American Triangle" setup seen here. It may be best to habitually avoid the American Triangle setup.

(**ABOVE**): Two bolts, clipped off with two quickdraws.

PRO. This is almost the perfect setup, the only way to anchor off to a bolt anchor – directly into the hangers.

CON. Almost nothing. Remember the tragic story of the climber on El Cap who clipped straight into a chain? A link broke, the rope whipped off the chain and the climber and his partners plunged to the next world. This is the only time I know for certain that an anchor chain has failed, though I'm positive there are other cases. Normal chain link is prone to metal fatigue after a couple seasons. I never liked hanging my hide off something I wasn't sure about, and it's nearly impossible to determine how good, or poor, a chain is. Unequivocally, this setup would be best if the bolts were connected with two shoulder-length slings twisted to form two parallel, redundant equalizing slings, with the rope attached to the slings with both a locking and non-locking carabiner, gates opposed. However, the setup shown is quick, and certainly adequate if both bolts are bombproof. A figure-eight knot would also be superior to this overhand knot.

Sources

U.S. Gear Manufacturers and Sources

Black Diamond Equipmemt, Ltd. 2084 East 3900 South, Salt Lake City UT   84124   (801) 278-5533

Blue Water   209 Lovvorn Road, Carollton GA 30117 (404) 834-7515

Climb High   1861 Shelburne Road, Shelbourne VT 05482 (802) 985-5056

Lowe Alpine Systems   Box 1449, Broomfield CO 80038 (303) 465-3706

Metolius Mountain Products   63255 Lyman Place, Bend OR 97701   (505) 382-7585

PMI   Box 803, LaFayette GA 30728 (800) 282-7673

SMC   12880 Northrup Way, Bellevue WA 98005 (206) 883-0334

Wild Country USA   624 Main Street, Conway NH 03818 (603) 447-1961

Yates Gear   1600 E Cypress Ave, Suite 8, Redding CA 96002 (916) 222-4606

Essential Reading

Each year's climbing accidents are compiled and published in *Accidents in North American Mountaineering*, available from mountaineering stores nationwide.

Supplemental Instruction

The American Mountain Guides Association is an excellent source of qualified instructors and guides. They can be reached at Post Office Box 2128, Estes Park CO 80517   (303) 586-0571.